D0127823

Five-Star Basketball Coaches' Playbook

Edited by Leigh Klein, Matt Masiero and Kevin Pigott

equilibrium
books
A Division of Wish Publishing

LCCN: 2004104117

Book edited by Leigh Klein, Matt Masiero and Kevin Pigott
Cover designed by Phil Velikan
Editorial assistance provided by Heather Lowhorn and Shay Berry

Printed in the United States of America
10 9 8 7 6 5 4 3 2 1

Published in the United States by
Equilibrium Books, A Division of Wish Publishing
P.O. Box 10337
Terre Haute, Indiana 47801, USA
www.wishpublishing.com

Distributed in the United States by
Cardinal Publishers Group
Indianapolis, Indiana 46268

Table of Contents

Introduction

When the Five-Star Basketball Camp was founded, it was not the intention of Howard Garfinkel and Will Klein to provide a place where coaches could perfect their craft. Their primary concern was to create a place where players could perfect their skills during the summer under the tutelage of some of the best teachers in the country. From those early days the camp has evolved into our current structure – daily teaching stations, lectures, and competitive games combined with "Station 13", our optional individual instruction period each day. Not only did our Stationmasters teach the game to the campers, but also they became mentors to the coaches. Five-Star Basketball Camp became the place to learn the craft of coaching.

In 1966 at Camp Orin Sekwa, NY, the first Five-Star staff included future NBA legends Hubie Brown and Chuck Daly. The influence of these coaching pioneers was evidenced in two ways. First, they became mentors to the other coaches on the staff. Second, they brought with them a group of young, energetic, and bright coaches who were soon to climb the coaching ladder. Former general manager of the Chicago Bulls, Jerry Krauss, pointed out that no other institution has had the influence on the game of basketball like that of the Five-Star Basketball Camp. Clearly it is pervasive throughout the NBA and NCAA. For example, currently there are 55 NCAA Division 1 head coaches that have worked the Five-Star Camp prior to ever coaching Division 1 basketball!

There is no doubt that the enthusiasm for the game of basketball has increased. At the Five-Star Basketball Camp, we continually see players from other countries coming to America to perfect their skills. The NBA draft is evidence enough of the international popularity of basketball. With this increased worldwide participation, the Five-Star Basketball Camp saw a growing hunger to learn how to play the game correctly. In 1987, our first book, *Five-Star Basketball Drills*, was published. Our goal was to provide both player and coach with a body of work that could help the player increase his or her basketball skills. Nearly 100,000 copies of the first edition have sold throughout the world. Since that time we have published other drill books to enhance the library of basketball enthusiasts. The *Five-Star Basketball Coaches' Playbook* is our attempt to provide coaches at all levels with an anthology of offensive plays to fit all their needs. It is a collection of favorite plays from our family of coaches. Some of the coaches you will recognize immediately. More importantly, however, is that all of the coaches presented here are true masters of the craft of coaching basketball.

The inspiration of this book is the dedication and creativity of all the coaches who have worked at Five-Star. They have done their internship at the Five-Star Basketball Camp working under "professors" such as Hubie Brown or Chuck Daly. Some of the products of their coaching careers can be found in this anthology. We are confident that they will assist you in your quest for basketball excellence.

Yours for Better Basketball,
Leigh Klein, Matt Masiero, and Kevin Pigott

Section One:
Man-to-Man Offense

Quick Hitter

Diagram 1

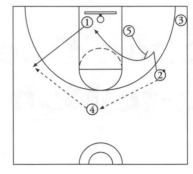

Diagram 2

Diagram 3

Diagram 4

Purpose:

To execute a quick hitter against a man-man defense.

Organization:

Player 1 enters the ball to player 2 on the wing. Player 3 empties to the ball side corner. Player 4 sets a back screen for player 1 who is looking for the lob from player 2 (diagram 1).

Variations:

• If the lob is not there, player 2 reverses the ball to player 4 at the top. Player 1 sprints out to the wing and receives the pass from 4. Player 5 steps out and sets a back screen for 2, who looks for post up in lane (diagram 2).

• Player 2 posts up on the ball-side block. Players 5 and 4 set a stagger double screen for player 3, who flashes from the opposite side corner (diagram 3).

• Finish play with player 2 stepping out to set a back screen for 5. Player 5 gets to ball-side block for post-up (diagram 4).

First look is into the post, second look is to player 3 for a three-point shot (diagram 3).

41

Diagram 1

Diagram 2

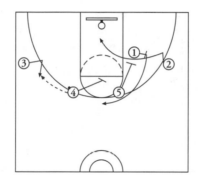

Diagram 3

Purpose:

To execute an effective dual (high/low) scoring opportunity against a man-to-man defense utilizing a 1-4 high alignment.

Organization:

Player 1 enters the ball to player 2 on the wing and cuts off player 5 on the ball side elbow to the low block (diagram 1). Player 2 reverses the ball to the player 5, who reverses to player 4 on opposite elbow (diagram 2). Player 4 passes to player 3 on the left wing, as player 1 back screens for player 2, and players 5 and 4 then stagger double screen for player 1 (diagram 3).

- Start in a 1-4 high alignment
- Player 3 can pass to player 2 who is cutting to block or to player 1 coming off the stagger double screen (diagram 3).

Zipper Fade

Diagram 1

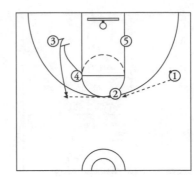

Diagram 2

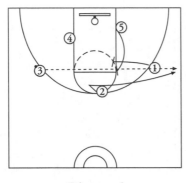

Diagram 3

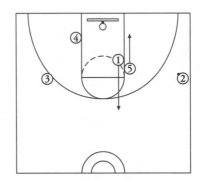

Diagram 4

Purpose:

To execute an effective dual (high/low) scoring opportunity against a man-to-man defense utilizing a 1-4 high alignment.

Organization:

Player 1 dribbles wing out, forcing player 2 to zipper up the lane. Player 5 downscreens for player 2 (diagram 1). Player 1 passes high to player 2, as player 4 downscreens for player 3. Player 2 then hits player 3 on the wing (diagram 2). Players 1 and 5 fade screen for player 2 (diagram 3). Player 5 then rolls down the lane. Player 3 looks to skip pass to player 2 on the wing, as player 1 clears high ready for reset (diagram 4).

Hot Tips

- Start in a 1-4 high alignment.
- Player 1 must pop to top after fade screen. Player 5 rolls down the lane to post (diagram 3).
- Player 3 hits player 2 for a shot or a pass down to player 5. Player 3 can also pass to player 1 at top to go into passing game (diagram 3).

42/43 & 42/43 Thumb

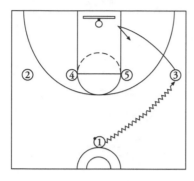

Diagram 1

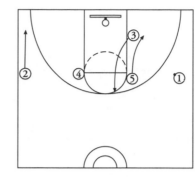

Diagram 2

Diagram 3

Diagram 4

Purpose:

To execute a series of effective man-to-man quick hitters utilizing the 1-4 high alignment.

Organization:

Player 1 dribbles to the side of players 5 and 3, as player 3 dives to the block (diagram 1). Player 3 zipper cuts off of player 5, who posts up on the right block. Player 2 dives from left wing to left corner (diagram 2). On a pass from player 1 to player 3, player 4 sets the wide down screen for 2 (diagram 3).

Variations:

* Thumb Play: Execute the same post and zipper cut by player 3 into "42/43." Player 1 passes to player 3 (diagram 5). Player 4 sets a high ball screen for player 3 (diagram 6). Player 4 rolls, as player 5 flashes and replaces player 4 at the top of the key (diagram 7).

* "42C" or Counter: If player 2 is over played, then player 2 goes the opposite way off of a screen from player 5, as player 1 clears through the middle (diagram 4).

* "42 Thumb" Counter: On a catch by player 3, player 5 clears to opposite side and player 3 fakes a screen from player 4 and drives to basket or draws and dishes to player 1 in the corner (diagram 8).

Diagram 5

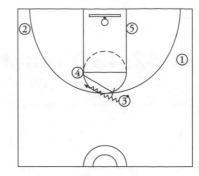

Diagram 6

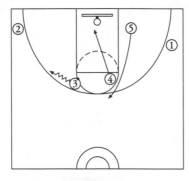

Diagram 7

Diagram 8

- "42" is when player 2 is receiving the screen from player 4.
- When faking use of the screen, player 3 must go hard toward player 4's screen and then utilize a crossover dribble to change direction and drive.

42/43 Thumb Down

Diagram 1

Diagram 2

Diagram 3

Purpose:

To execute an effective counter to the 42/43 Thumb 1-4 high offense set.

Organization:

This play starts like "42" (see previous play) as player 1 dribbles toward player 3, who zippers off of player 5 to the top of the key, and receives the pass from player 1 (diagram 1). On the pass to player 3, player 4 comes over to screen (diagram 2). Player 5 clears to weak side block as player 3 fakes use of the screen and drives into a draw and dish situation with player 1 or 5 (diagram 3).

- When faking use of the screen, player 3 must go hard toward player 4's screen and then utilize a crossover dribble to change direction and drive.
- Player 1 penetrates deep enough to get a good passing angle to player 1 or 5.

Kansas

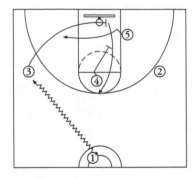

Diagram 1

Diagram 2

Purpose:

To execute an effective scoring option for the screener.

Organization:

Player 1 dribbles the ball to the left wing. Player 3 goes from the left wing and screens for player 5 on opposite block. Player 4 down screens for player 3, the screener (diagram 1). Player 5 cuts off the screen from player 3 and posts ball-side block. Player 3 dives to the basket as player 4 fills the top (diagram 2).

Variation:

- If player 5 is unavailable, then player 1 reverses the ball to player 4 and looks for 3 posting.

Hot Tip Player 1 must drive the ball to the wing hard as the action is coming from the opposite side.

UMass

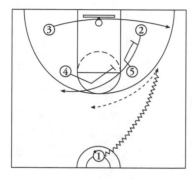

Diagram 1

Diagram 2

Purpose:

To execute an effective scoring option for player 2.

Organization:

Players 5 and 4 set a stagger-double down screen for player 2. Player 3 cuts (clears) from the left side to right corner. Player 4 opens up to the ball after setting the screen looking for a pass. Player 1 dribbles to the right wing and passes to player 2 (diagram 1). Player 2 receives the pass from player 1 and looks for shot or drives the ball to left wing. Player 4 dives to the block on a player 2 dribble. Player 5 flashes to high post after down screen (diagram 2).

Variation:

• If player 2 does not get an initial shot after stagger double screen, then player 2 drives hard to the left wing. Player 4 drives hard to ball-side block and player 5 flashes hard to high post.

Player 2 must come off stagger double screen looking for the shot. If there is no shot, then player 2 must take it hard to opposite wing and let play develop for player 4 or 5.

3 Spin

Diagram 1

Diagram 2

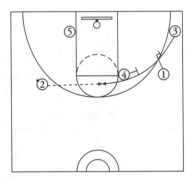

Diagram 3

Diagram 4

Purpose:

To execute a man offense out of a box set.

Organization:

Players 3 and 2 set up on the left and right block. Players 5 and 4 set up at the left and right elbows. Player 1 dribbles hard to the right wing, as player 3 cuts hard to the right corner and player 2 flashes from the right block to the top of the key. Player 1 passes to 2 (diagram 1). If player 2 receives the pass from player 1, player 5 walks defender down from the elbow, spins, and posts up when player 2 creates a 45-degree angle for post entry pass (diagram 2). If player 5 posts, players 4 and 1 set a stagger double screen for player 3 coming out of the corner. Player 2 passes to 3 (diagram 3).

Variations:

- If player 5's defender is side fronting or full fronting, hit player 2 off the double screen and player 5 seals for the lay-up.

Player 5 must cut hard and the entry pass must be thrown away from the defense.

Kentucky

Diagram 1

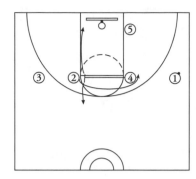

Diagram 2

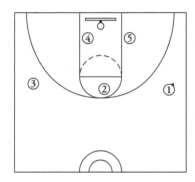

Diagram 3

Purpose:

To execute a set play that exploits both inside and outside scoring opportunities.

Organization:

Player 1 dribbles to the right wing, forcing player 2 to make a basket cut. Once player 2 gets to the low block, 2 then back screens for player 5. Using the back screen, player 5 v-cuts to the ballside block. Player 1 looks to feed the player in the low post (diagram 1). After player 2 sets the screen for player 5, player 4 screens for player 2. Player 1 looks to pass to player 2 or 4. Player 4 must read player 2. If player 2 curls to the basket, then player 4 pops out high. If player 2 stays high, then player 4 rolls to the basket (diagram 2). If no scoring opportunities occur, then use 3-out, 2-in motion principles (diagram 3).

Variation:

• Can be run on either side.

Hot Tip Player 4 must have good timing on the screen for 2.

Storm

Diagram 1

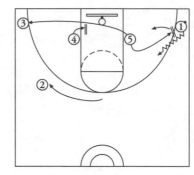

Diagram 2

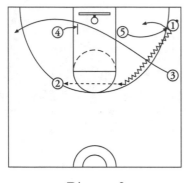

Diagram 3

Diagram 4

Purpose:

To execute a man-man offense that utilizes the triangle alignment concept.

Organization:

Player 3 passes to player 1 in the ball side (right) corner and makes an inside baseline cut looking for pass back from 1. Player 5 flashes up to ball-side post (diagram 1). If no ball side action is available, player 1 dribble penetrates off a pick from player 5 and skip passes to player 2 (diagram 3). Player 2 catches and dribble penetrates from top of key to left wing, as player 3 is deep in the ball-side corner and player 4 is posting ball side block (diagram 4).

Variation:

If player 2 cannot execute the give-and-go pass with player 3, 3 cuts all the way to the opposite corner, player 1 dribble penetrates to the baseline for the jump shot or executes a screen-and-roll with player 5. Player 2 fans out to the opposite wing (diagram 2).

Hot Tips

- Initial set is with player 2 at top of key, player 4 left block, 5 ball-side block, 1 ball-side corner and 3 has ball on right wing.
- Corner series of options.
- Pass and cut or use screens.

Twirl

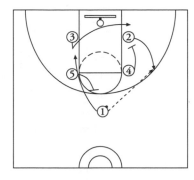

Diagram 1

Diagram 2

Diagram 3

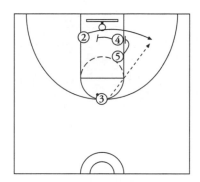

Diagram 4

Purpose:

From an initial box set, set up player 2 for a shot after a continual screening game.

Organization:

Player 1 passes the ball to player 2 on the right wing after a down screen from player 4. Player 5 backscreens for player 1, after pass to player 2. Player 3 flashes to ball-side short corner (diagram 1). Player 2 reverses to player 5, who reverses to player 1 on left wing. Player 2 then shuffle cuts off player 4's screen to the ball side block (diagram 2). Players 4 and 5 then set a stagger-double down screen for player 3, who comes off to the top (diagram 3). Players 4 and 5 then set a stagger-double cross screen for player 2, who is cutting hard to ball side corner (diagram 4).

Hot Tips

- This is a box set, where players 5 and 4 set up in the left and right high post elbowsand players 3 and 2 are set up on the left and right blocks.
- Player 2 must cut hard off each screen.
- Players 4 and 5 must set consecutive stagger double screens (down and then cross).

13

Two-Play

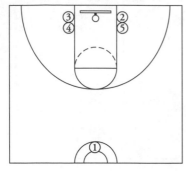

Diagram 1

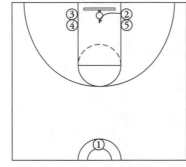

Diagram 2

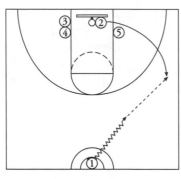

Diagram 3

Diagram 4

Diagram 5

Diagram 6

Purpose:

To execute a man-man offensive quick-hit play that can lead into motion.

Organization:

Players start in a double stack on the low blocks. Players 5 and 2 on the right side and players 4 and 3 on the left side for the two-play (diagram 1). If "2" is called out, then player 2 goes to the middle of lane, setting up the defense (diagram 2).

• Option #1 *Single Screen* – Player 2 comes off single screen from player 5 and pops out to the right wing. Player 1 passes to 2 (diagram 3). Player 5 screens away to opposite block for player 4, as player 1 down screens for player 3 after pass is made to player 2 (diagram 4).

- Option#2 *Double Screen* – Player 2 comes off of a double screen from players 4 and 3 and pops out to the left wing. Player 1 passes to 2 (diagram 5). Players 4 and 3 then set a double cross screen for player 5, as player 1 down screens for player 3 after passing to player 2 (diagram 6).

- On the initial call player 2 must read the defender and determine whether it will be a single or double screen used.
- Option #1 *Single Screen* – Player 4 man posts hard to ball-side block and player 3 pops up to elbow or the top of the key.

Three-Play

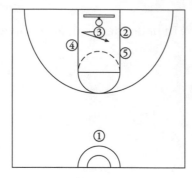

Diagram 1

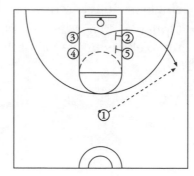

Diagram 2

Diagram 3

Diagram 4

Diagram 5

Purpose:

To execute a man-man offensive quick-hit play.

Organization:

If "3" is called out then player 3 goes to the middle of lane, setting up the defense (diagram 1).

• Option #1 *Double Screen* – Player 3 comes of a double screen from players 5 and 2 and pops out to the right wing. Player 1 passes to 3 (diagram 2). Players 5 and 2 then set a double cross screen for player 4, as player 1 down screens for 2 after a pass to 3 (diagram 3).

- Option #2 *Single Screen* – Player 3 comes off single screen from player 4 and pops out to the left wing. Player 1 passes to 3 (diagram 4). Player 4 screens away to opposite block for player 5, as player 1 down screens for player 2 after pass is made to 3 (diagram 5).

Hot Tips

- Three-play is like the two-play, but run for player 3.
- On the initial call, player 3 must read the defender and determine whether it will be a single or double screen used.

Stu Lash
Denver Nuggets

Strong Side Elbow Action

Diagram 1

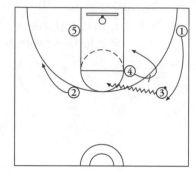

Diagram 2

Purpose:

To execute a man-to-man offense that utilizes screens from post to perimeter players.

Organization:

Player 1 hits player 3 on the right wing, cuts to the corner in front of player 3 . Player 3 looks to player 5 for a lob pass after a backscreen from player 2 (diagram 1). If there is no lob pass, player 4 sets a ball screen for player 3 and pops to the mid-post area. Player 2 pops out for a three-point shot after the backscreen.

Player 3 drives hard after the ball screen from player 4. Player 1 loops back for defensive balance.

Direct Post Play

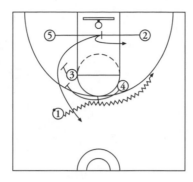

Diagram 1

Purpose:

To execute a man-man offense that utilizes screens from post to perimeter players.

Organization:

Player 1 penetrates to the right wing off a ball screen from player 4. Player 2 cross screens for player 5. If player 1 cannot pass to player 5 in the post, player 2 continues through after screen for 5 and receives a stagger double screen from player 3, then player 4 for a 3-point shot at top.

Every screen is a big on small, so if there is a switch it creates a mismatch.

Horns

Diagram 1

Diagram 2

Diagram 3

Purpose:

To execute a man-to-man screening offense.

Organization:

Player 5 sets a ball screen for player 1, then dives to left block. Player 1 comes off a ball screen from player 5 to the right wing. Player 2 clears out from the right block to left block. Player 3 flashes from left baseline to mid-post extended area (diagram 1). Player 1 reverses to player 4 at the top of key. Player 2 comes off a down screen from player 3 to the left wing. Player 5 sets a screen for player 3, who goes makes a flex cut to the right block (diagram 2). After the reversal from player 4 to player 2, 4 immediately cross screens for player 1 coming to the top and then receives a back screen from player 3 (diagram 3).

Hot Tips

- The initial set up has players 4 and 5 outside the 3-point line, player 2 is on the right block and player 3 in the left short corner area.
- Player 2 has multiple options: pass to player 1 at the top for a shot or hit player 4 going to basket off a back screen (diagram 3).

Rockets

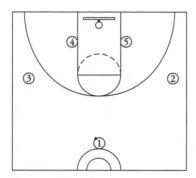

Diagram 1

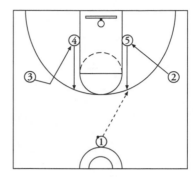

Diagram 2

Diagram 3

Diagram 4

Purpose:

To execute a man-man motion offense that utilizes a 3-out 2-in set.

Organization:

The play starts with 3-out 2-in set up: players 2 and 3 on wings, player 1 at top and players 4 and 5 on blocks (diagram 1). Players 4 and 5 flash to the elbows and look for pass. Simultaneously, players 2 and 3 cut back door going all the way to opposite side blocks. Player 1 passes to 5 (diagram 2). Player 5 has ball and player 1 cuts off behind 5 for possible handoff. Player 4 down screens for player 2, who receives the pass from player 5 (diagram 3). Player 4 sets a baseline screen for player 3, who comes to ball side corner and receives a pass from player 2. Player 4 up screens for player 5. Player 5 rolls ball side post (diagram 4).

Variations:

Player 3 can take shot or pass to player 5 in low block (diagram 4).

Hot Tips

- Player 1 must cut off hard for hand-off (diagram 3).
- Player 4 must stay and set screen for player 3, then up screen for player 5 (diagram 4).

21

Wichita

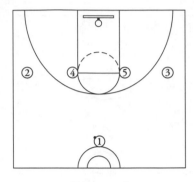

Diagram 1

Diagram 2

Diagram 3

Purpose:
  To execute a man-man offense that is out of a box set.

Organization:
  Start with a box set: players 2 and 3 on elbows, player 1 at top and players 4 and 5 on blocks (diagram 1). Player 3 ballscreens for player 1 and rolls back to the top. Player 2 goes to ball-side corner off a stagger-double back screen from 5 and 4 (diagram 2). Player 1 reverses to player 3 at the top. Player 5 ballscreens for player 3 and rolls to the basket. Player 4 pops out to top (diagram 3).

Variation:
  Player 1 can take it to the basket; hit player 5 on the roll or player 4 on the pop out (diagram 1).

Hot Tip

Player 4 must pop out and create space for player 5 to roll to basket (diagram 3).

Zebra

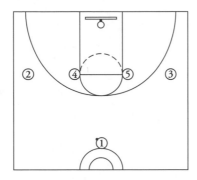

Diagram 1

Diagram 2

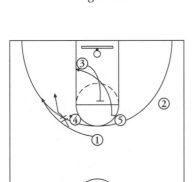

Diagram 3

Diagram 4

Purpose:

To execute a man-to-man offense that utilizes a 1-4 high alignment and gets an open shot for the screener.

Organization:

Star with 1-4 high set up: players 2 and 3 are on wings, players 4 and 5 on elbows, and player 1 is at top (diagram 1). Player 4 back screens for 2, who cuts over the top to right wing. Player 1 passes to player 4. Player 3 cuts from right wing to left block (diagram 2). Player 4 hands off to player 1, as player 3 flashes up to back screen for player 5 in the high post (diagram 3). After hand-off, player 4 down screens for 3. Player 1 looks to pass to player 3 for shot (diagram 4).

Box

Diagram 1

Diagram 2

Purpose:

Designed to execute a screen play out of a box entry into 4-out motion.

Organization:

Player 1 will enter the pass to player 3 on the right wing, after a diagonal cut off player 4. Player 1 will then shallow cut to ball-side corner. Player 5 goes to the left side block and waits for player 2's cross screen (diagram 1). Player 5 uses player 2's screen and goes to right block. Player 4 will set a down screen for player 2. Player 2 will then pop to the key area as player 4 goes to the left corner (diagram 2).

Variation:

After player 2 comes off double screen and is behind the 3-point line, player 3 releases to curl off player 5's screen to the weak side elbow for a jump shot. Player 4 steps in lane, turns back around, and seals, posting up (diagram 2).

Hot Tip Will run box into 4-out motion series.

Tony Staffiere
Regis College

Hometown Isolation

Diagram 1

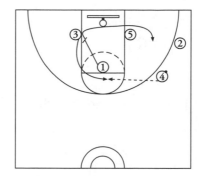

Diagram 2

Purpose:

Designed to get players a 1-on-1 isolation on any side of the court.

Organization:

Player 1 passes to player 4 on the right wing as player 2 cuts diagonally through the middle to ball-side corner (diagram 1). Player 1 screens down for player 3 and moves to the right short corner. Player 3 catches pass and creates a 1-on-1 situation toward basket (diagram 2).

Variation:

Can be run for any player.

- The play takes on many names based on the player it is run for. For example, "Boston" is the verbal call if the player is from Boston.
- Ball is entered on the side that the player who the play is run for is on.

Reggie

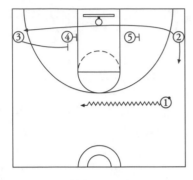

Diagram 1

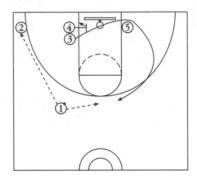

Diagram 2

Purpose:

To execute an effective man-man quick hitter that utilizes the 3-point shot, has a counter, and is initiated from a 1-4 low alignment.

Organization:

Play starts in a 1-4 low. Player 2 flashes up to receive the pass from player 1, but cuts off of player 5's back screen, and then players 3 and 4 set a double block screen. Player 1 fakes the pass to player 2 on right wing and then penetrates to left (diagram 1).

Variation:

After player 2 comes off double screen and is behind the 3-point line, player 3 releases to curl off of player 5's screen to the weak side elbow for a jump shot. Player 4 steps in lane, turns back around, and seals, posting up (diagram 2).

- Player 1 can hit player 2 in the corner for shot or hit player 3 curling to weak side elbow.
- Player 2 can take shot or pass into player 4 on ballside block.

Lob-Flex

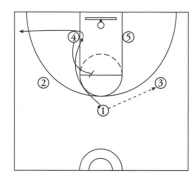

Diagram 1

Diagram 2

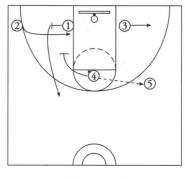

Diagram 3

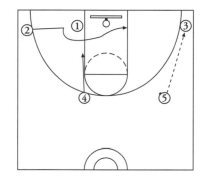

Diagram 4

Purpose:

To execute a quick hit man-man offensive set play into flex.

Organization:

Player 1 passes to player 3 and then runs off a back screen from player 4. Player 3 looks for the lob pass to player 1 (diagram 1). If player 1 does not receive the lob pass from player 3, 1 clears to the left corner. Player 4 flashes to receive the middle, top of key for pass from player 3. Player 5 back screens for player 3, as player 2 cuts down to set a curl screen for player 1 (diagram 2). If player 4 can't hit player 3 going back door or player 1 on the curl to the block, 4 reverses the pass to player 5 and 1 back screens for player 2, as the flex offense is initiated (diagram 3). Player 5 passes to player 3 as player 2 cuts to right block. Player 4 downscreens for player 1. This is the flex offense (diagram 4).

Hot Tips

- Player 2 sets the curl screen and must fade to left corner for spacing and flex (diagram 2).

- Once player 4 passes to player 5, player 3 must fade to corner for spacing and player 2's cut on the flex (diagram 3).

9

Diagram 1

Diagram 2

Diagram 3

Purpose:

To execute a man-man offense that utilizes screens to free up your best shooter.

Organization:

Player 1 uses a ball screen from player 5. Player 4 posts up hard on the right block (diagram 1). After the screen for player 1, player 5 then sets a walkaway screen for player 3 (diagram 2). Player 1 reverses the ball to player 3. Player 2 comes from right wing off a stagger double screen from player 4 (right block) and player 5 (left wing) (diagram 3).

Variations:

• If player 2 has no shot, look for player 5 posting up.

• Or if player 2 has no shot, reverse back to player 3 for shot.

Hot Tips

• Player 2 is your best shooter.

• Player 5 sets down screen for player 2, shapes up to the ball and then seals, posting up (diagram 3).

Flare

Diagram 1

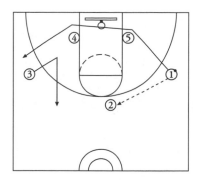

Diagram 2

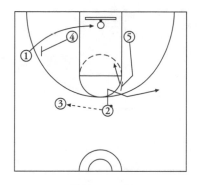

Diagram 3

Purpose:

To execute a scoring opportunity off a flare-screen.

Organization:

Player 1 dribble drives to the right wing. Player 2 is dribble chased by player 1 from the right wing and cuts off a screen from player 5 to the top of the key (diagram 1). Player 1 reverses the ball to player 2 and immediately cuts to the rim and continues to the left corner. Player 3 cuts hard to receive the next pass (diagram 2). Player 2 reverses the ball to player 3 and then receives a flare screen from player 5. Player 4 back screens player 1. Player 5 cuts and dives after flare screen for player 2 (diagram 3).

Hot Tip

Player 1 must hold cut until player 5 releases off a flare screen for player 2 (diagram 3).

29

Ballscreen

Diagram 1

Diagram 2

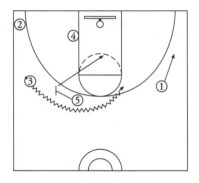

Diagram 3

Purpose:

To execute a scoring opportunity score off a ballscreen.

Organization:

Player 1 initiates the offense from the right side and passes to player 4 at the top of the key. Player 4 receives the pass from player 1 and reverses to the player 3 on the left wing (diagram 1). As player 3 receives pass, player 2 cuts to the ballside corner and player 4 down screens for player 5 (diagram 2). After a down screen from player 4, player 5 sets a ball screen for player 3 (diagram 3).

Variations:

- Player 3 either dribbles hard off a screen from player 5 (diagram 3), or tries to get to the rim.
- Draw help from player 1's defender and pass to 1 for shot, or pass to player 5 on the roll, or pass back to player 4.

Hot Tip Timing of screens (set and use) is crucial!

Give and Go

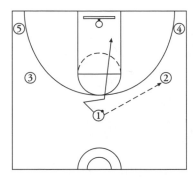

Diagram 1

Diagram 2

Diagram 3

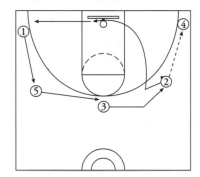

Diagram 4

Purpose:

To execute a man-man offense that focuses on passing and screening away and cutting to the basket.

Organization:

After entering the ball, player 1 takes one step away like he is going to set a screen. Player 1 v-cuts toward player 3 and then makes a hard basket cut all the way down the middle of the lane (diagram 1). As player 1 vacates the top area, player 3 must fill from the left wing and player 5 must fill the left wing from the left corner. After the cut, player 1 fills the left corner, which is the open area (diagram 2). Player 2 reverses the ball to 3 at the top of the key, cuts toward player 4 as if to screen and then makes a basket cut down the middle of the lane. Player 4 fills to same side wing and player 2 fills offside corner (diagram 3).

Variations:

- *Pass to the Corner*: After receiving the pass from player 1 on the initial set play, player 2 immediately passes to player 4 in ball side corner, takes a step toward player 3 as to screen and then makes a hard cut toward basket on the right wing. Player 2 then must fill the opposite side as every other player fills one spot ahead (diagram 4).

- *Corner-Out*: This is the one time that player 4 must fill out to ball side, as player 3 filled one spot ahead. After diagram 4, player 4 passes to 3 on ball-side wing and then v-cuts toward basket,

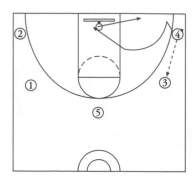

Diagram 5

Diagram 6

replacing oneself in ball-side corner (diagram 5).

- *Flares*: Player 1 can pass to player 2 on the right wing and receive a back screen from player 3 and flare to the left wing (diagram 6).

- *Flares*: After player 2 receives the pass from player 1; they it back to player 3, receive a back screen from player 4, and then flare to the corner (diagram 7).

Diagram 7

- The only way to set up the give-and-go is to first teach the concept of passing and screening away.
- Defense will expect the screen away, and then you can give and go with surprise and effectiveness.
- Any time the defense overplays, make a back cut to the basket.
- Move the ball, move people, screen!

Shandu

Diagram 1

Diagram 2

Diagram 3

Diagram 4

Purpose:

To execute a man-man offense that is initiated from a low double stack alignment and exploits the baseline dribble drive, draw and dish.

Organization:

Player 1 passes to player 3 off a double stack. Player 4 comes from the low block all the way to the top of the key. Player 2 comes off of player 4's backside straight to the foul line. After the pass to player 3, player 1 jab steps and misdirects toward player 2, then cuts hard toward player 3 (diagram 1). Player 3 will jab step toward the baseline, then dribble full speed toward the top, and player 1 will come behind for a handoff or short pass. Player 2 will be set at the elbow asking for the ball (decoy). Player 4 remains high above the top of key. Player 3 will flip the ball to player 1, then go straight off of player 2's pick at the foul line. Player 5 flashes to the strong side corner on the pass to player 3 who is also asking for the ball (diagram 2). Player 5 is already in the corner as player 3 received the ball to clear out the paint. As soon as player 1 gets the ball from player 3, 1 dribbles toward the basket and pulls up, as 3 will pop open off player 2's pick for a lob or easy lay-up (diagram 3).

- Player 1 should be clearing toward player 3 by the time player 4 reaches the top.
- Player 2 must seal off and ask for the ball at the elbow, which will draw the defender (X2) from the bottom.
- These are secondary options if the defense switches.

Low-High

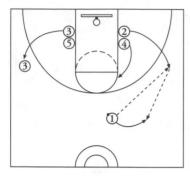

Diagram 1

Diagram 2

Diagram 3

Diagram 4

Purpose:

To execute a man-man offense that initiates from a low double-stack set.

Organization:

Player 5 picks for player 3 to get open on the wing and player 4 picks for player 2, player 4 then rolls to the elbow asking for the pass from or 1 (decoy). Player 4 acts as a decoy. Player 1 makes the pass to player 2 on the wing, and then frees him for a return pass (diagram 1). Player 2 makes a back door cut after passing back out to the top to player 1. Player 4 down screens to the opposite block for player 5 (who comes up to the ball-side elbow), then pops out above the arc on the left side for a pass from 1 (diagram 2). Player 5 down screens for player 2, who pops out to the right wing. Player 1 cuts down the middle of the lane, continuing to the left side, receiving a down screen from player 3. Player 4 pass fakes to 2 and then passes to player 1 on the left wing (diagram 3). Player 3 rolls out to the corner after setting the down screen for player 1 (asking for the ball as a decoy). Player 5 will cross the lane and back pick for player 4 on the ballside elbow. Player 4 comes off back screen, looking for a lob pass from 1. Player 2 comes to the top of key for defensive balance (diagram 4).

Variation:

If pass from player 1 to 4 is not there, player 5 needs to seal high postman and roll to the basket.

Hot Tips

- Player 4 is a decoy for return pass.
- Lob pass from player 1 to 4 will be there!
- Player 3 is a decoy.

High

Diagram 1

Diagram 2

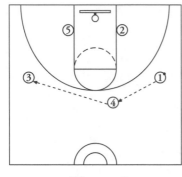

Diagram 3

Diagram 4

Purpose:

To create an easy scoring opportunity that is initiated from a 1-4 high alignment and will develop open looks near the rim, three-point area or isolation in the post.

Organization:

Initial set up as follows: players 2 through 4 line up high across the foul line extended. Your best leaper is player 4, your best shooter is player 2 and your best post player is player 5 (diagram 1). Player 1 dribbles into the right wing forcing player 3 to go baseline off a stagger double screen by player 2 on strong-side block and player 5 on weak side block (diagram 2). Player 4 pops out to the top of the key area outside of the three-point line. Player 1 reverses the ball to player 4, who quickly continues the reversal to player 3 (diagram 3). Player 2 sets a back screen for player 4 and steps out beyond the three-point line. Player 4 cuts to the basket looking for a lob pass from player 3. Player 1 gets back as defensive safety, as this will help to keep the defender high to ball level and away from the helpside near the hoop (diagram 4).

Variations:

If the lob pass is not open, player 3 passes to player 2 for a three-point attempt (diagram 5). If the pass to player 2 is not available, then player 3 can make a post entry pass to player 5 for a one-on-one isolation (diagram 6).

Diagram 5

Diagram 6

• Make sure player 4 sets up his man on the back screen. Player 3 should lob the pass high to the opposite side of the rim for player 4 to go retrieve it and dunk the ball (if possible).

• Player 2 should set the screen and open immediately to the ball for a quick opportunity to shoot a three-point shot (diagram 5).

• Player 5 should set the screen and open to the ball immediately because the dump down to the post might be available as a first option before the lob (diagram 6).

Greg Collins
University of Louisville

N.B. Eagles

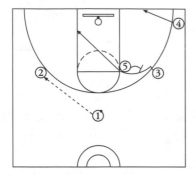

Diagram 1

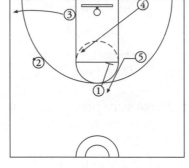

Diagram 2

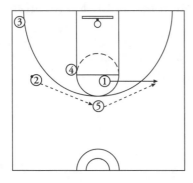

Diagram 3

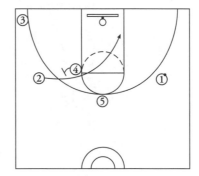

Diagram 4

Diagram 5

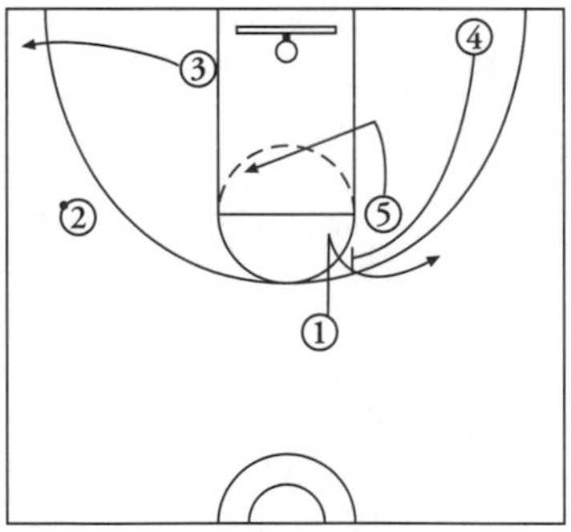

Purpose:

To create 1-on-1 opportunities, leading to high percentage shots.

Organization:

- Option 1: *Basic 3 cut* (everything is based on player 3's cut) – As player 1 passes away from player 5's side of the floor, player 3 cuts into the lane off player 5's screen. Player 4 works toward baseline (diagram 1).
- Option 2: *Player 4 flashes into the lane* – Player 3 clears the post if it is not a good opportunity. Player 1 down screens for player 5 or 5 can flare screen for 1, creating a skip pass for a 3-point shot (diagram 2). The wing player 2 can restart the continuity by passing to player 5 at the top of the key. Player 2 can also do this by utilizing a backup dribble (diagram 3). Now the continuity stars on the opposite side. Player 2 cuts through the lane off a back screen from player 4 (diagram 4).

Variation:

The post option: Player 2 slides down the lane after screening for the cutter, looking for opportunity to pop into the lane. Players 4 and 1 interchange or player 4 can set a flare screen for 1. The wrinkle will maintain continuity, but keep the post (player 5) from leaving the lane area (diagram 5).

- All five players play all positions.
- Requires patience, discipline, and execution.
- All five players must be able to handle.
- Brings the post player out on the floor.
- Requires 1-on-1 play.
- Anytime you can beat your defender to the basket – that is the play!
- High percentage shots.

Creighton

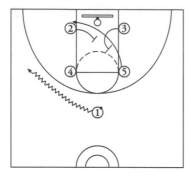

Diagram 1

Diagram 2

Purpose:

To execute an effective man-to-man, quick hitting offensive play that initiates from a box set and utilizes a screen the screener concept to exploit both a post and perimeter scoring opportunity.

Organization:

Player 1 dribbles to the wing while players 2 and 3 back screen for 5. Player 5 cuts to ballside post (diagram 1). Player 3 pops out to opposite wing while player 4 down screens for 2 (diagram 2).

Variation:

Player 1 looks to pass to player 5 who is posting ballside block or to player 2, coming to top. Player 3 might be available for a skip pass if defender sags to help on defense. If neither a post entry nor a skip pass is available, player 4 cuts to basket off of 2's back screen (small to big screen).

Hot Tips

- Initial set up includes player 1 with the ball at the top of the key, player 4 on the left elbow, 5 on the right elbow, player 2 on the left block and 3 on the right block.
- Timing of the staggered screens is very important!

Green/Green-44

Diagram 1

Diagram 2

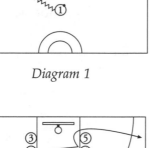

Diagram 3

Diagram 4

Diagram 5

Purpose:

To execute an effective man-man, quick hitting offensive play that initiates from a double stack (low) and utilizes a back door and curl cut to exploit both a perimeter and post scoring opportunity.

Organization:

Initial set up: Player 1 is at the top with the ball; stack has players 4 and 5 (high and low) on the left side and players 2 and 3 (low and high) on the right side. Player 1 dribbles toward 4 and 5. Player 2 now cuts off the stack (4 and 5) under player 5 to receive pass in the left corner, looking for a one-one scoring opportunity (diagram 1).

If player 2 is not open, player 3 flashes up to the right elbow and, if open, receives a pass from 1 for a shot. If player 3 is overplayed on the elbow, he makes an immediate back door cut for a lay-up (diagram 2).

Variation:

"Green-44": Player 1 is at the top with the ball, players 4 and 5 are on the right side and players 2 and 3 are on the left side. Player 1 dribbles toward right wing, signaling player 2 to cut off the stack (players 4 and 5). Player 2 moves under 5 to receive pass in the right corner, looking for a one-one scoring opportunity (diagram 3). Player 3 begins to pop up to the left, midpost lane area before the pass from player 1 to 2. When player 2 receives the pass from 1, players 4 and 5 double screen in the lane for 3 (diagram 4). Player 3 cuts over the top of player 4, curling to the ballside block for a pass and score from player 2 (diagram 5).

Hot Tips

- Player 1 declares a side of the floor and dribbles to the guard spot. Player 2 catches the ball and must look to score (diagram 1).
- "Green-44" – Initial "Stack" set up is opposite of "Green." Player 1 dribbles away from 2 and 3 (diagram 3).
- Player 3 must stay outside the lane for spacing and hold position about three-quarters of the way up the lane, before the curl (diagram 4).
- Player 3 must make a tight curl off of 4 and get to the block for a lay-up or short jump shot (diagram 5).

Duquesne

Diagram 1

Diagram 2

Diagram 3

Diagram 4

Purpose:

To execute an effective man-to-man, quick hitting offensive play that initiates from a box set and utilizes three sets of staggered double screens to exploit two perimeter scoring options.

Organization:

Player 1 starts with the ball above the foul line extended, dribbles hard at both elbows using the ball screens set by players 4 and 5, and comes to the left wing (diagram 1). Player 4 and then 5 stagger screen for player 2, popping out to the top to receive a reversal pass from player 1 (diagram 2). Player 4 and then 5 set another stagger baseline screen for player 3, who curls to receive a pass from player 2 looking to score (diagram 3).

Variation:

If player 3 is not open for the shot, player 3 looks to 4 who is in the ballside short corner or to player 5 in the ballside midpost (diagram 4).

Hot Tips

- After player 4 sets the initial screen for player 3, he fades to the short corner. After 5 sets the second screen for 3 who pops to the midpost area.
- Timing of the staggered screens is very important.

Trotter

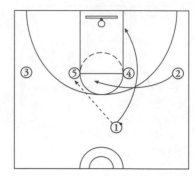

Diagram 1   Diagram 2

Purpose:

To execute an effective man-man quick hitter that initiates out of a 1-4 high alignment, utilizes X-cut action on the ball and will lead into flex, motion or any half-court offense.

Organization:

Player 1 passes to 4. Players 1 and 2 then X-cut off 4 with player 2 coming off high to the free throw line and player 1 going off low to the corner. Player 3 cuts down from wing and receives a downscreen from 5, who turns and posts, ducking in to the lane (diagram 1).

Variation:

Instead of passing to player 4, 1 can pass to player 5, and players 1 and 2 can make the X-cut off player 4.

- Initial set up is with player 1 with the ball at top of key (right lane side), player 2 is on the right wing, player 4 on right elbow, 5 on left elbow and player 3 on left wing.
- The X-cut is very tough to defend. Defenses that switch still have trouble because player 4 can screen and seal defenders.
- Guarding 5, you have no weak-side help.
- Options:
  - Player 4 can handoff pass to player 1 or 2 making the X-cut.
  - Player 4 can hit 3 on the left wing, who can hit 5 posting.
  - Player 4 can pass to 5, who seals and then ducks in after screen for 3.

Wrap

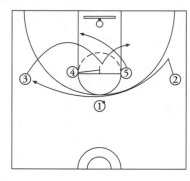

Diagram 1

Diagram 2

Purpose:

To execute an effective man-to-man quick hitter that initiates out of a 1-4 high alignment, utilizes a screen the screener concept, and will lead into flex, motion, or any half-court offense.

Organization:

Player 1 dribbles over to the right wing. Player 2 cuts over the top to the left wing off a stagger double screen from player 5 then 4 and receives a reversal pass from 1. Player 3 immediately cuts down and flashes up to backscreen player 5, who rolls off left block and posts up (diagram 1).

Hot Tips

- Initial set up is with player 1 at top of the key with the ball (right lane side), 2 is on right wing, 5 is on right elbow, 4 is at left elbow and 3 is on left wing.
- Player 5 must turn and make a hard cut off of 3's screen as player 1 reverses the ball to 2 on the left wing (diagram 2).

Detroit

Diagram 1

Diagram 2

Purpose:

To execute an effective man-man quick hitter that initiates out of a 1-4 high alignment, utilizes a pick and roll and will lead into flex, motion or any half-court offense.

Organization:

Player 1 passes to player 2 and cuts down the lane, looping through to the right corner. Player 4 now steps across to execute a pick and roll with player 2. On the opposite side, player 3 v-cuts down the sideline and then flashes hard to set a flare screen for player 5 (diagram 1).

Variation:

After pass to player 2, player 1 can clear out or come back up and back screen for player 4, looking for the lob (diagram 2).

Hot Tips

- Initial set up is with player 1 at the top of the key with the ball (right lane side), 2 is on right wing, 4 is at right elbow, 5 is at left elbow and 3 is at left wing.
- When player 3 flare screens for 5, this will clear out weak side help defender.
- Options:
    - Players 2 and 4 execute the pick and roll.
    - Player 2 passes to 4 for the lob (after back screen from player 1).
    - Player 2 passes to 5 flaring off of player 3's screen.

Pick and Pitch

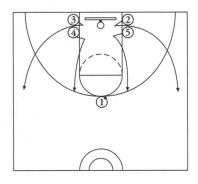

Diagram 1

Diagram 2

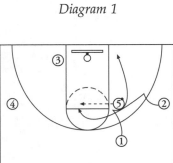

Diagram 3

Diagram 4

Purpose:

To execute an effective man-man offense that initiates from a double low stack into a 1-4 high alignment and exploits numerous scoring opportunities utilizing pick and pitch options.

Organization:

Players initiate from a double low stack with players 2 and 5 (top and bottom) on the right side and 3 and 4 (top and bottom) on the left side. With player 1 at the top of the key, the players break into a 1-4 high set, with 2 on the right wing, 5 on the right elbow, 4 on the left elbow and 3 on the left wing (diagram 1). Player 1 dribbles toward the right and makes a pass to 5 on the right elbow. Simultaneously, player 3 cuts down from left wing to block, as 4 flashes from left elbow to left wing, replacing 3 (diagram 2). After pass to player 5, player 1 cuts toward the basket, outside the lane, and off 5's hip. Player 2 views 1 cutting and then makes own cut off of 1's backside, coming to the middle free throw lane area, and receiving a pitch pass from player 5 for a shot (diagram 3).

Variation:

If player 2 is not open, 4 down screens for player 3 (who pops out to the left wing), and seals defender on the left block (diagram 4). Player 2 has two options:

- Pass to player 3 on the left wing for a shot
- Pass to player 4 on left block for a score.

Lee University

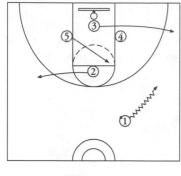

Diagram 1

Diagram 2

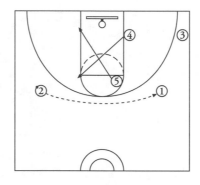

Diagram 3

Purpose:

 To execute an effective man-man offense that utilizes perimeter skip passes and high/low action from the post players.

Organization:

 Player 1 dribbles toward the right wing. Player 3 pops out to ballside corner. Player 2 cuts to opposite wing from free throw line. Player 5 flashes to ballside elbow from midpost area (left side). Player 4 post up on right block (diagram 1). Player 1 can pass to 3 or to 5 in the high post. Player 4 seals defender on right block (diagram 2). Player 1 skip passes the ball to 2 on the left wing. On the pass, players 4 and 5 cross looking for high/low action (diagram 3).

Variation:

 If player 5 gets the pass from 1, 5 looks to player 4 sealing the defender.

Hot Tips

- Players 4 and 5 perform X action, with player 4 flashing from right, low block to left, high post (elbow) and 5 diving from right, high post (elbow) to low, left block (diagram 3).

Gold

Diagram 1

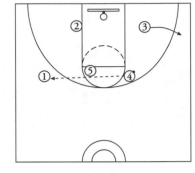

Diagram 2

Diagram 3

Diagram 4

Purpose:

To execute an effective man-man offense that is initiated from 1-4 alignment and utilities post and perimeter screens.

Organization:

Player 2 cuts down to left block, as player 1 passes to 4 on the right elbow, then cuts off of player 5's flare screen to the left wing. Player 3 back door cuts from right wing. Player 4 looks to 3 cutting back door (diagram 1). Player 4 passes to 1 coming off of 5's flare screen, as 3 continues through to right corner after not receiving the pass from 4. Player 2 is at the left block (diagram 2). Players 4 and 5 set a double down screen for 2, popping out to the top of key, looking for the shot (diagram 3).

Variation:

If player 2 has no shot, then 2 reverses the ball to 3 on the right wing and then interchanges with 1. Player 4 posts up on right block, screens away for 5 (who cuts to ball-side block), then flashes to high post/free throw line (diagram 4).

Hot Tip

Player 2 has set up the cut, as the ball was skip passed from 4 to 1 (diagram 3).

Gold Special

Diagram 1

Diagram 2

Diagram 3

Diagram 4

Purpose:

To execute an effective man-man offense that is initiated from 1-4 alignment and utilizes screen the screener concepts, exploiting post and perimeter scoring options.

Organization:

Same action as "Gold" (diagram 1). Player 4 skip passes to 1, as player 5 pops out high. Player 3 widens out from right block to right wing (diagram 2). Player 2 sets a diagonal screen for 4 in the high post. As player 2 is up screening for 4, 5 comes down to screen for 2 (diagram 3).

Variation:

If player 2 has no shot, then 2 reverses the ball to player 3 on the right wing and then interchanges with 1. Player 5 posts up on right block, screens away for player 4 (who cuts to ballside block). Player 5 then flashes to high post/free throw line (diagram 4).

Hot Tips

- Initial set up is as follows: player 1 starts with ball at the top of the key, player 3 is on the right wing, player 2 is on the left wing, player 5 on left elbow and player 4 on right elbow.
- Player 2 has set up the cut, as the ball was skip passed from player 4 to 1 (diagram 3).

Fresno/Fresno 2

Diagram 1

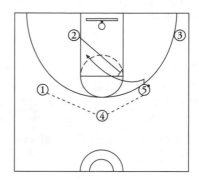

Diagram 2

Diagram 3

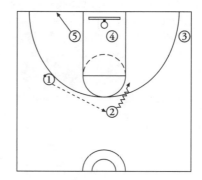

Diagram 4

Diagram 5

Diagram 6

Purpose:

This set provides two opportunities to get ball to low post with small and big screens.

Organization:

Player 1 makes an entry pass to 5 and receives backscreen from 4. Player 1 makes flare cut. Player 3 cuts to right corner (diagram 1). The ball is quickly reversed from player 5 to 4 to 1. Player 2 sets diagonal backscreen for 5 (small to big emphasis). Player 5 waits for and reads screen to cut to ballside low post (diagram 2). Player 1 will attempt a post entry for 5. Player 3 might be available for a skip pass if his defender sags off him to help on defense. If neither a post entry nor a skip pass is available, player 4 cuts to basket off of 2's backscreen (small to big screen [diagram 3]). Player 1 reverses the ball to 2, who dribbles hard at the right elbow (diagram 4). Player 4 spins and pins his defender after coming off of 2's initial screen. Player 2 feeds 4 for shot. Player 2 must read to see if 3's defender helps (diagram 5).

Diagram 7

Variations:

- In "Fresno 2," all action is the same until player 2 sets back screen for 4 (diagram 3). Player 4 comes off the backscreen and continues across the lane in order to set a screen for 5, who is in the opposite block. Player 5 cuts low (diagram 6).

- Player 2 dribbles hard to right elbow and looks for 5 or 4 who should both be in "hi-lo" after 4's screen (diagram 7).

Hot Tip

Player 5 must read 4's cross screen and decide to go either low or high. Player 4 must react and go opposite.

Michigan

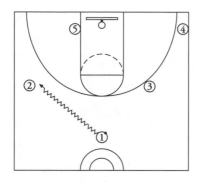

Diagram 1

Diagram 2

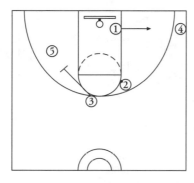

Diagram 3

Diagram 4

Purpose:

Set play with dribble handoff, ball screen, and two screens off the ball. A "big to small screen" and a "small to big screen" are used to create mismatches when the defense switches.

Organization:

Player 1 dribbles to wing and hands off to 2 (diagram 1). Player 2 dribbles hard to top of the key, where he receives ball screen from 3. After handoff from player 2, 1 receives backscreen from 5 (diagram 2). Player 2 looks for 1 in low post area off of backscreen. Player 3 continues across and downscreens for 5. Player 3 must be quick! If player 1 is not open in post area he continues out to backscreen for 4 (diagram 3). Player 2 has passing options from either one of two screens. Player 1 can pass to 5 who has curled off of 3's downscreen. Player 2 can pass to 4 coming off of 1's backscreen. Of course, player 2 can also hit screeners 1 or 3 who now will spot-up after setting their screens. The middle of the floor might open up with this screening action. If so, player 2 will have a one-on-one opportunity (diagram 4).

Initial set up is as follows: player 1 has the ball at the top of the key, player 2 is on left wing, player 3 is on right wing, player 4 is in the right corner, and player 5 is on the left block.

Cutter/Roll Back

Diagram 1

Diagram 2

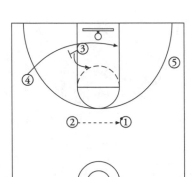

Diagram 3

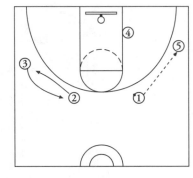

Diagram 4

Purpose:

To execute an effective man-man offense that is initiated from a box set and utilizes screening, cutting and roll back offensive concepts.

Organization:

Player 1 dribbles to the right, as player 5 down screens for 3. Player 4 sets an "L" screen for player 2 (who pops out to top) on the left block (diagram 1). Player 1 passes to 2, as player 5 backscreens for 3, then rolls back to middle of lane (diagram 2). As player 2 reverses the ball to 1, player 3 backscreens for player 4, then rolls back to the middle of the lane (diagram 3).

Variation:

If player 1 passes to 5, then players 2 and 3 exchange (diagram 4).

Hot Tips

- Initial set up is as follows: player 1 starts with the ball at the top of the key, player 4 is on the left wing, player 5 is on the right wing, player 2 is on the left block and player 3 is on the right block.
- After player 4 sets the "L" screen, 4 pops back out to left wing (diagram 2).
- After player 5 backscreens, 5 pops back out to wing.
- After setting backscreens, screener must roll back to lane.

Cutter/Roll Back-Counter

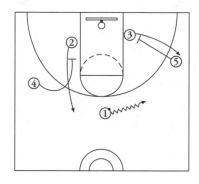

Diagram 1

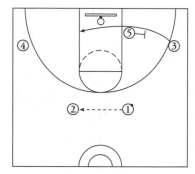

Diagram 2

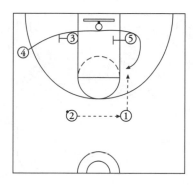

Diagram 3

Purpose:

To execute an effective man-man offense that is initiated from a box set and utilizes a double backscreen for a post scoring option.

Organization:

Player 1 dribbles to the right, as player 5 downscreens for 3. Player 4 sets an "L" screen for 2 (who pops out to top) on the left block (diagram 1). Player 1 passes to 2, as player 5 backscreens for 3 (diagram 2). As player 2 reverses the ball to 1, player 4 curls off a backscreen from 3 and then player 5, popping out to the middle post area for a shot on the right side (diagram 3).

- Initial set up is as follows: player 1 starts with the ball at the top of the key, player 4 is on the left wing, player 5 is on the right wing, player 2 is on the left block and player 3 is on the right block.
- After player 4 sets the "L" screen, 4 pops back out to left wing (diagram 2).
- After player 5 backscreens for player 3, 5 stays at right block to set the second backscreen for player 4.
- After setting backscreens, screener must roll back to lane.

Down

Diagram 1

Diagram 2

Diagram 3

Purpose:

To execute an effective man-man offense that is initiated from "5-out set" and looks to isolate the post player inside.

Organization:

- Option 1 – Player 1 dribbles toward player 2 on the right wing, initiating 2 to cut back door and continuing through to screen for 5 in the middle of lane. As player 4 pops up to right wing, replacing 2, 1 passes to 4. Player 5 cuts to ballside block looking for ball (diagram 1).
- Option 2 – If player 5 is not open, player 1 V-cuts and repositions to receive pass from 4. On the pass player 3 sets a cross screen for 5. Player 2 pops out to the left wing, receives the reversal pass from 1, and immediately looks inside for 5 (diagram 2).

Variation:

If player 5 is not open, player 1 downscreens for 3, (who pops out for a three-point shot) and receives a pass from 2 (diagram 3).

Initial set up is as follows: player 1 is with the ball at the top of the key, player 2 is on the right wing, player 4 is in the right corner, player 3 is on the left wing and player 5 in the left corner.

Hand off/Hand off Opposite

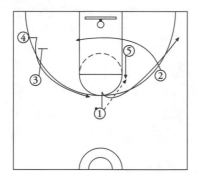

Diagram 1

Diagram 2

Diagram 3

Diagram 4

Purpose:

To execute an effective man-man offense that utilizes hand off options for the post players, creating a perimeter isolation opportunity.

Organization:

Player 5 flashes to the right elbow, high post area and receives the pass from player 1. Simultaneously, player 2 cuts from right wing to the left block. Player 1 then cuts off 5 looking for the hand off. Player 3 is down screening for 4, who flashes to the opposite high post area for a second hand off opportunity (diagram 1). Player 5 now hands off to player 4, as 4 attacks the defense (diagram 2).

Variations:

- Player 1 passes to 5 in the high post and screens away for player 3, who slips the screen and cuts to the basket. Player 2 V-cuts and comes to 5 for a dribble hand off (diagram 3).

- Player 3 pops to corner, as 2 attacks the middle with a dribble. Player 5 dives to the right block after hand off to 2 (diagram 4).

- When player 5 catches the pass from player 1, 5 must fake the hand off, taking care of the ball so the defense doesn't steal it. This sets up the second hand off to player 4 (diagram 2).

Flyers

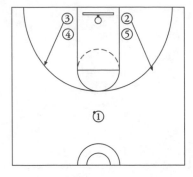

Diagram 1

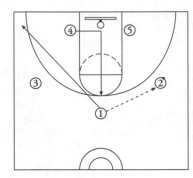

Diagram 2

Diagram 3

Diagram 4

Purpose:

To execute an effective man-man offense that initiates out of a double stack, utilizes screen the screener options and exploits a low post and perimeter scoring opportunity.

Organization:

Offense initiates out of a double stack with players 2 and 3 popping out to the right and left wings off screens from 5 and 4 (diagram 1). Player 1 passes to player 2 on the right wing and cuts to opposite baseline. As 1 is cutting, player 4 makes an "L" cut up the lane to high post (diagram 2). Player 2 reverses the ball to player 4 and 4 has a few options (diagram 3):

• Player 4 looks to 5 for high/low action.

• If the high/low action is not available, then player 3 cuts back door, looking for pass, and setting up next action. Player 4 reverses the ball to 1 on the left wing, as player 3 cross screens for 5, who cuts to left block and posts, and 4 downscreens for 3, who pops out top for shot (diagram 4).

Variation:

If player 3 is not open on the back door cut, player 1 v-cuts to get open on the left wing (diagram 3).

Hot Tip

As player 4 realizes that player 5 is not open, 4 pump fakes, signaling 3 to cut back door (diagram 3).

45

Diagram 1

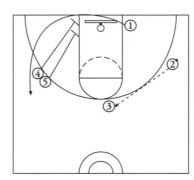

Diagram 2

Diagram 3

Purpose:

To execute an effective man-man offense that initiates out of a double stack (post and perimeter), utilizes a low post scoring opportunity.

Organization:

As player 2 pops out to the right wing off the low stack to receive a pass from player 1, player 3 flashes up to the right elbow to set a backscreen for 1, who cuts to right block (diagram 1). Player 3 steps out and receives a reversal pass from 2. Players 4 and 5 set a double downscreen for player 1, who has continued through after passing to 2 (diagram 2). Player 3 dribbles to the left and passes to 1 on the left wing. Player 1 looks for shot or inside to post, as player 4 curls over the top off 5's back screen. Then player 5 steps to the ball (diagram 3).

Hot Tip Initial set up is as follows: Player 1 is at the top of the key with the ball, players 2 and 3 are stacked (low/high) on the right block and players 4 and 5 are stacked (side by side) on the left wing.

4 High

Diagram 1

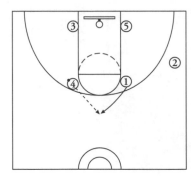

Diagram 2

Diagram 3

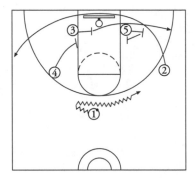

Diagram 4

Purpose:

To execute an effective man-man offense that initiates out of a 1-4 high alignment and utilizes a triple stagger screen to exploit scoring options for player 2.

Organization:

Player 1 passes to player 4 on the left elbow and then screens for player 5 on the right elbow. Player 3 immediately cuts back door from left wing looking for pass from 4. Player 5 curl cuts off of 1's screen and goes to right block (diagram 1). After screening for 5, player 1 pops back out to top and receives a pass from 4 (diagram 2). Players 5, 3, and 4 set a triple stagger screen for player 2, who has cut from right wing to left corner, looking for the shot (diagram 3).

Variation:

Player 1 can change direction with a dribble and pass to player 3, who comes off a screen from player 5 (diagram 4).

- Initial set up is as follows: Player 1 is at the top of the key with the ball, player 2 is on the right wing, player 5 on the right elbow, player 4 on the left elbow and player 3 on the left wing.
- After screening for player 2, player 5 must turn on the block and re-screen for 3 (diagram 4).

Ball Screen

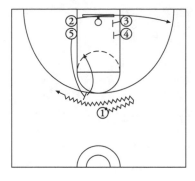
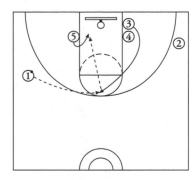

Diagram 1	*Diagram 2*

Diagram 3

Purpose:

To execute an effective man-man offense that initiates out of a double stack and utilizes a high/low post pass entry and a pick and roll to exploit scoring opportunities.

Organization:

Out of the stack, player 2 comes off a double screen from players 3 and 4, misdirecting to the right corner. Simultaneously, player 5 flashes up to the left elbow, executing a pick and roll with 1 (diagram 1). On the right block, player 3 cuts off the back of 4 to the high post (free throw line) area to receive a pass from 1. Player 3 looks to 5, on a high/low feed (diagram 2).

Variation:

If player 3 does not pass to 5, player 4 flashes up to right elbow to execute a pick and roll with 3 (diagram 3).

- Initial set up is as follows: player 1 is at the top of the key with the ball, players 2 and 5 are stacked (low/high) on the left block and players 3 and 4 are stacked (low/high) on the right block.
- Player 1 must dribble clear to the left wing, and player 5 must roll to the left block so the next action can take place (diagram 1).
- After posting off the roll, player 5 must step over and seal the defender on the pass from player 1 to 3 (diagram 2).

Peoria

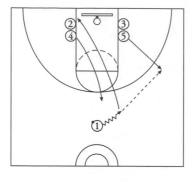

Diagram 1

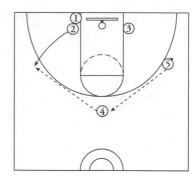

Diagram 2

Diagram 3

Purpose:

To execute an effective man-to-man offense that is initiated out of a double stack and utilitzes a double stagger screen and a screen the screener concept for both a low post and perimeter scoring opportunity.

Organization:

Player 5 pops out to the right wing to receive a pass from player 1, who then cuts through the middle of the lane to the left block. Simultaneously, player 4 flashes to the top (diagram 1). Player 5 reverses the ball to player 4, and on the catch, player 2 pops out to receive the reversal from player 4 (diagram 2). Players 1 and 3 set a double staggered screen for player 5, who cuts to the left ballside block. At the same time, player 4 is screening for player 1 who will come to the top of the key after the first part of the stagger screen for 5. Player 2 looks to hit player 5 in the low post, then looks to hit player 1 at the top (diagram 3).

Hot Tips

- Initial set up is as follows: Player 1 is at the top of the key with the ball, players 2 and 4 stacked (low/high) on the left block, players 3 and 5 are stacked (low/high) on the right block.
- Player 2 must wait for player 4 to catch the ball from player 5 before popping out to the wing (diagram 2).

John Saintignon
Canyon del Oro High School

Wing

Diagram 1

Diagram 2

Diagram 3

Diagram 4

Diagram 5

Diagram 6

Purpose:

To execute an effective man-man offense that utilizes a 1-4 alignment with multiple options and continuity.

Organization:

Player 1 has the ball and can go to either side, players 4 and 5 set up on either elbow and players 2 and 3 either wing (diagram 1). Player 1 passes to 2 on the wing, as player 5 clears to opposite elbow (diagram 2). After pass to player 2, 1 makes a face cut to the basket, looking for the return pass from 2. Simultaneously, players 4 and 5 set a double screen for 3, who either cuts off the back of player 1 to low block or high to top of key(diagram 3). If the pass does not go to player 3 on the low block, 3 continues to corner. Player 5 returns to top or key looking for reversal from 2. Player 4 sets a down screen for 1 and posts up (diagram 4). Player 1 pops out to the left wing after down screen from 4. Player 2 sets the beginning of stagger double screen for 3 in the corner, as player 5 reverses the ball to 1 and sets the second screen for 3. Player 5 then rolls to the right block as 3 comes to the top of key (diagram 5). Player 1 looks to enter to 4 in low post. Continuity starts if 1 reverses the ball to top of key with players 4 and 5 flashing to the elbows (diagram 6).

Variations:

This play can be executed on both sides of the floor.

Once player 5 sets the second screen for player 3 and rolls to the hoop, 5 looks for the lob pass from player 1 (diagram 5).

Niagara

Diagram 1

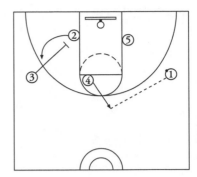

Diagram 2

Diagram 3

Purpose:

To execute an effective man-man offense that utilizes a 1-4 alignment exploiting both a low post and perimeter scoring option.

Organization:

Player 1 dribbles toward 2, as player 2 clears to weakside block. Player 4 cross screens for player 5 on opposite elbow and rolls to ballside block looking for pass from 1 (diagram 1). Player 4 steps out for reversal pass from 1. Player 3 downscreens for 2 on opposite block (diagram 2). After player 2 receives a pass from 4, player 3 cross screens for 5 and then comes off a downscreen from 4. Player 2 looks to pass to 5 and then to player 3 (diagram 3).

Hot Tip   Initial set is 1 at top, 2 on the right wing, 5 on right elbow, 4 on left elbow and 3 on left wing.

Peter Wolf
Santa Fe Community College

Dorado

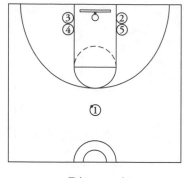

Diagram 1

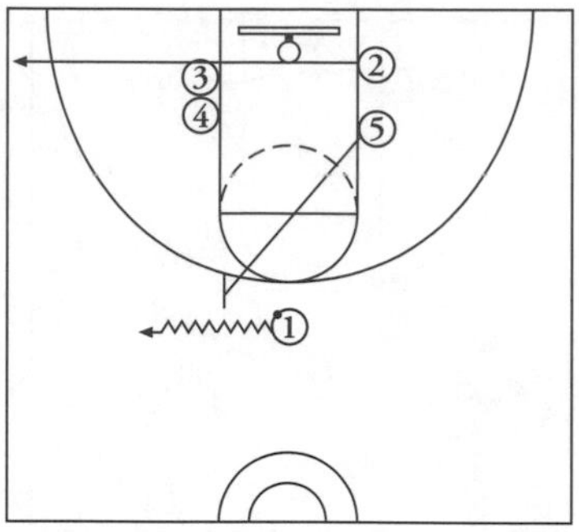

Diagram 2

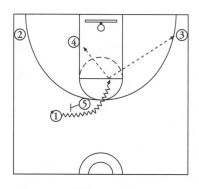

Diagram 3

Purpose:

To execute an effective man-to-man offense that utilizes the low double stack set up.

Organization:

Intial set up is as follows: players 2 and 5 are on the right side, and players 3 and 4 are on the left side in a double stack (diagram 1). Player 1 dribbles across to the best shooter for a corner three-point range shot. Player 2 flashes to the left corner off a double screen from 3 and 5. After 2 breaks, player 5 cuts to the top of the key to sets a screen and roll with player 1 (diagram 2). Player 3 goes across to the opposite three-point corner after 2 comes off player 3's shoulder. Player 4 posts up.

Variations:

- If open for the shot, player 1 passes to player 2 in the corner or 4 in the post (diagram 3).
- If not open for the shot, player 1 keeps dribbling, crosses over, uses 5's screen and roll and drives to the basket. Player 1 will penetrate and put up a lay-up or down pass to player 4 who will pitch to 3 in the corner or to 5 who has rolled (diagram 3).

Cutter-4

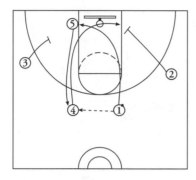

Diagram 1

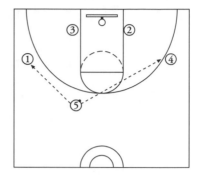

Diagram 2

Purpose:

To execute an effective man-man offense that has multiple options.

Organization:

Players 4 and 5 make simultaneous cuts, with 4 going to ballside block and 5 to top of key. Player 1 passes to 5, cuts down the lane to left block and then receives a back screen from player 3. Player 2 sets a down screen for player 4 after 4 has cut through (diagram 1). Player 5 has the ball (diagram 2) and several options:

- Option 1: Player 5 can pass to player 1, who can shoot the jump shot or pass to player 3 opening up in the low post after screen for 1. If player 5 passes to 1, 5 screens away for player 4.
- Option 2: Player 5 reverses the ball to 4, who is reading the defender off the down screen from Player 2. Player 5 then screens away for player 1.

Variation:

If player 4's defender collapses on player 1 cutting, then 4 will be open for a shot in the corner (diagram 2).

Hot Tips

- Initial set up is as follows: players 1 and 4 are a lane width apart at the top of the key. Players 3 and 2 are on the left and right wings, and player 5 is on left block.
- Player 5 has the ball and will pass to player 4, who either curls for a jumper or fades to corner based on defender.

Duke

Diagram 1

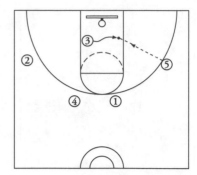

Diagram 2

Purpose:

To execute an effective man-man isolation quick hitter out of motion.

Organization:

Player 5 back screens for 3 (who cuts into lane) on the right wing and then pops out to receive the pass from 1. Player 4 backscreens for 2 on the left wing (diagram 1). Player 3 cuts back from middle of the lane to receive pass back from 5 for isolation in lane (diagram 2).

Hot Tips

- Initial set up is as follows: player 1 attacking from top of key, 2 is at left side top, 3 right wing, 4 left wing and 5 right block.
- Player 3 must make a cut off the backscreen as to go all the way to other side, but immediately cut back to ballside (diagram 1).

Triangle

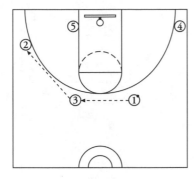

Diagram 1

Diagram 2

Diagram 3

Purpose:
   This is a quick hit play versus a man-to-man that creates a backscreen for a lay-up.

Organization:
   Player 1 brings the ball up and passes to 3. Player 3 passes over to player 2 on the left wing (diagram 1). Player 2 dribbles at 3 for a handoff as they interchange. Player 5 flashes from ballside block to ballside elbow (diagram 2). Player 2 makes an inside cut down the lane off a backscreen from player 5. Player 3 passes to 2 for a lay-up (diagram 3).

Hot Tips

- Initial set up is as follows: Players 1 and 3 are a lane width apart at the top of key, player 5 is at left block, player 2 left wing and player 4, the right corner.
- Player 2 must set the defender up and then cut hard for a lay-up (diagram 3).

Corner

Diagram 1

Diagram 2

Diagram 3

Diagram 4

Purpose:

To get quick shot verses a man-man defense utilizing the 2-3 alignment.

Organization:

Initial set up is a 2-3 set. Players 1 and 2 are the guards (two guard front), players 3 and 4 are the wings (left & right, respectively), and 5 is the post player (diagram 1). Player 3 v-cuts to get open and receive pass from 1, who shallow cuts ball-side corner. On the pass, player 5 flashes to ball-side elbow (diagram 2). Player 3 passes to 1 in the corner and makes a hard basket cut, looking for the return pass (diagram 3). Once player 3 is in the lane and does not receive the pass back from player 1, 5 dives hard toward 1 and executes a pick and roll. Simultaneously, player 3 continues through and receives a stagger double downscreen from 4 then 2. Player 1 can drive, shoot the jumper, pass to 5, or pass to 3 (diagram 4).

Hot Tip   When passing to wings and corners, passer should cut hard and look for return pass.

23-Flex

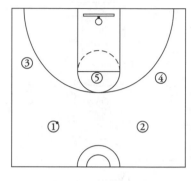

Diagram 1

Diagram 2

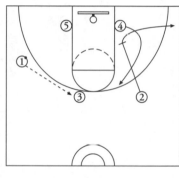

Diagram 3

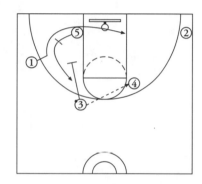

Diagram 4

Purpose:

To utilize a multipurpose offense that can result in a quick hitter or the flex offense.

Organization:

Initial we use a 2-3 set. Players 1 and 2 are the guards (two guard front), players 3 and 4 are the wings (left and right, respectively), and player 5 is in the high post (diagram 1). Player 1 dribbles toward 3 on the left wing. Player 3 cuts down toward the lane, flashes up, backscreens for player 5 at the high post and steps out to top key. Player 5 rolls to ball-side rim. 4 slides down to block (diagram 2). If player 5 is not open, then player 1 reverses the ball to 3, as player 2 downscreens for 4 coming to top, and then fades to corner (diagram 3). Player 3 reverses the ball to 4. If player 4 does not shoot, we start the flex offense: player 5 backscreens for player 1, who flex-cuts baseline, player 3 downscreens for 5 coming to the top (diagram 4).

1-3-1 Man Offense Dribble Down Options

Diagram 1

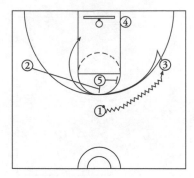

Diagram 2

Diagram 3

Purpose:
   To execute an effective man-man that utilizes a 1-3-1 set with a dribble down option.

Organization:
   Initial set up is as follows: Player 1 has the ball and can dribble at either player 2 (left wing) or 3 (right wing). Player 4, who is in the low post will always come ballside (diagram 1). As player 1 dribbles at 3, player 3 fakes down and then goes over the top of a double screen set by players 2 and 5. Player 1 looks down to 4, then to player 3 cutting to basket (diagram 2).

Variation:
   If player 1 cannot pass to 4 or 3, player 2 pops out after screen and receives the pass from 1. Player 2 may have the jump shot or can pass to player 3, who has curled back to the ball for a one-one isolation. Player 5 screens down for player 1 as a final option (diagram 3).

Hot Tips

• Can be executed from either side of the floor.
• Utilize all options.

Butler

Diagram 1

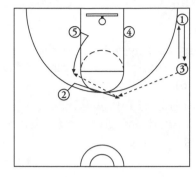

Diagram 2

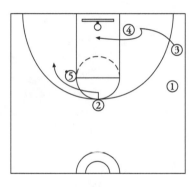

Diagram 3

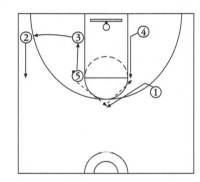

Diagram 4

Diagram 5

Diagram 6

Purpose:

To execute an effective man-man offense that utilizes various screens from the post players and scoring options for the cutting guards.

Organization:

Player 1 gets to an attack area and passes the ball to 3. Player 1 j-cuts through to the ballside corner. Player 4 comes off a backscreen from player 5 to ballside block looking for pass from 3 (diagram 1). Player 2 cuts and receives a pass from 3. Player 5 flashes up the lane and receives the pass from 2 on left elbow. Player 3 cuts baseline, as 1 cuts up to wing (diagram 2). Player 2 cuts off of 5. When needed, player 3 cuts ballside block off a backscreen from 4 (diagram 3). Player 1 cuts to top and receives the reversal pass from 5. Player 4 cuts up the lane and receives the pass from 1. Player 3 pops off of left block to corner area, as 5 drops down to replace 3. Player 2 cuts up to left wing (diagram 4). Player 1 cuts off of 4. When needed, player 3 cuts ballside block off a backscreen from 5, looking for pass from player 1. Pattern continues (diagram 5).

Variations:

- We call any cutting action off the high post player with the ball "five-way" basketball. It can be a dribble-off situation, where player 2 can receive pass back from player 5 and run a pick and roll (diagram 6).
- Initial set up is as follows: Player 1 attacks from the right side of half-court. Player 2 is on the left elbow extended past the top of key, player 3 is on right wing, player 4 is in the left corner and player 5 is left block.

Player 1 dribble attacks from the top, going hard and forcing the defense to guard 1.

Miami

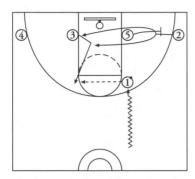

Diagram 1

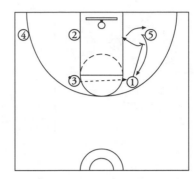

Diagram 2

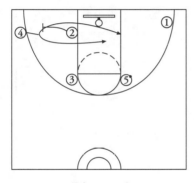

Diagram 3

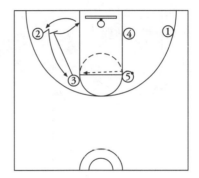

Diagram 4

Purpose:

To execute effective man-man continuity offense that initiates from a 1-4 low alignment and utilizes various back and down screens to create a dual scoring options (elbow jump shot or low post).

Organization:

Player 1 dribble attacks and reverses the ball to 3. Player 2 uses 5 for a screen and cuts baseline. Player 5 then widens out (diagram 1). Player 1 downscreens for 5, who pops out to right elbow. Player 3 passes to 5 or 1, sliding in the lane after screen. If the pass goes to 1, then 1 widens out (diagram 2). Player 4 uses 2 for a screen and cuts baseline. Player 2 then widens out (diagram 3). Player 3 downscreens for 2, who pops out to left elbow. Player 5 passes to 2 or 3, sliding in the lane after screen. If pass goes to player 2, then 2 widens out (diagram 4).

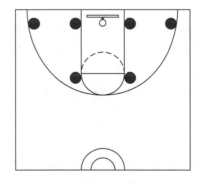

Diagram 5

 Hot Tips
- Initial set up is as follows: Player 1 attacks from the right side of half-court. Player 2 is ballside corner, 5 ballside block, 3 opposite block and player 4, opposite corner.
- Players will always be on or moving to 5 of these 6 spots (diagram 5).

4-Man Passing Game

Diagram 1

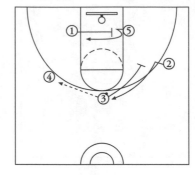

Diagram 2

Diagram 3

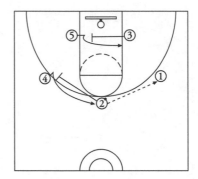

Diagram 4

Purpose:

To execute effective man-man continuity offense that emphasizes the pass and screen away concept from the perimeter and post players. This initiates out of a box set.

Organization:

Player 2 passes to 3 at the top of key. Player 1 then downscreens for 4, who comes to left elbow (diagram 1). Player 3 passes to 4 on the wing. Player 1 screens across for 5. Player 3 interchanges with 2 (diagram 2). Player 4 reverses the ball to 2 at the top, as player 3 downscreens for 1. Pattern continues (diagram 3). Player 2 passes to 1, and screens away for 4. Player 3 cross screens for 5, who comes to ballside block looking for pass from player 1 (diagram 4).

Hot Tips

- Initial set up is as follows: Player 2 is on the right wing with the ball, player 3 is at top of key, player 5 on the ballside block, player 4 is the opposite block and player 1 is on left wing.

- All interchanges are screens (diagram 2).

Fist

Diagram 1

Diagram 2

Purpose:

To execute an effective man-man set offense that initiates from a box set.

Organization:

Player 1 dribbles to right wing. Player 4 screens across for 5 on the left elbow. Player 2 up screens for player 5, as 5 cuts to ballside block (diagram 1). Players 2 and 4 set a stagger double screen for 3, coming to the top. Player 1 can hit 5 down low, player 3 off the stagger double screen or 4 rolling back to ball after screen for player 5 (diagram 2).

- Initial set up is at follows: player 1 at top, players 5 and 4 on left and right elbow, respectively, and players 3 and 2 on the left and right block, respectively.
- Player 4 sets screen for player 5 and must roll back hard to player 1 for pass option (diagram 2).

Zipper

Diagram 1

Diagram 2

Purpose:

To execute an effective man-man set offense that initiates from a box set.

Organization:

Player 1 dribbles to 5's side. Player 5 steps up and sets a ball screen for 1. Player 1 dribbles off player 5's screen to the right wing, as player 2 back screens for 4 cutting to low block (diagram 1). After player 2 sets a back screen for 4, 2 turns and sets the first part of the stagger double screen for 3. Player 5 then sets the second part of the stagger double for 3. Player 1 can hit player 3 at the top, 5 coming back to ball or 4 in low ball-side block (diagram 2).

- Initial set up is at follows: player 1 at top, players 5 and 4 on left and right elbow, respectively, and players 3 and 2 on the left and right block, respectively.
- Player 4 is always the player getting the back screen. Player 1 always dribbles away from 4 (diagram 2).

Army

Diagram 1

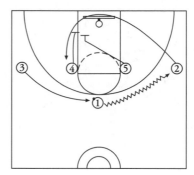

Diagram 2

Diagram 3

Purpose:

To execute an effective man-man set offense that utilizes the 1-4 high alignment to set stagger double screens for the shooter (player 2).

Organization:

Player 1 dribbles away from 2. Players 4 and 5 set a stagger double screen for 2. Player 3 cuts ballside corner as player 1 comes toward 3 on the dribble. Player 1 looks for 2 over the middle (diagram 1).

Variations:

• Player 1 dribbles toward player 2 as 2 cuts to opposite block and receives a stagger double screen. Player 3 flashes to point from left wing (diagram 2).

• Player 1 reverses the ball to player 3 at the top, who passes to player 2 coming off the stagger double screen (diagram 3).

Hot Tip Initial set up is as follows: player 1 at the top, players 4 and 5 at the elbows and players 3 and 2 on the wings.

Post

Diagram 1

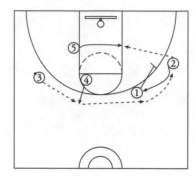

Diagram 2

Diagram 3

Purpose:

To execute a man-man offense that utilizes a quick hitter for both post players (4 and 5) cutting off back screens.

Organization:

On ball reversal (2-1-5-3), player 4 comes across and sets a back screen for player 5, who cuts to the basket looking for a quick score (diagram 1). If player 5 does not get the pass from 3, player 4 pops out to the top, as player 1 screens away for 2. Player 5 follows the ball, seals the defender and looks for a pass from player 2 (diagram 2). If player 5 can't get the quick entry, 5 sets an upscreen for player 4, who makes a basket cut. 5 holds the screen and flashes back to the ball (diagram 3).

- Initial set up is as follows: Player 2 starts with the ball on the right wing, player 1 is on the right sideline, player 5 is at the top of they key (left side), 3 on the left wing and player 4 on the right block.
- When coming off backscreens, post players must cut hard and seal defenders in low post.

Iso

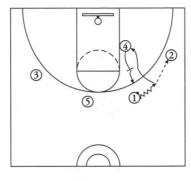

Diagram 1

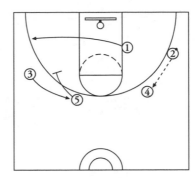

Diagram 2

Diagram 3

Purpose:

To execute an effective man-man offense that isolates a strong, quick guard and exploits numerous scoring options.

Organization:

Player 1 passes to player 2 and cuts off of 4's backscreen for the quick give and go or post isolation (diagram 1). If player 1 doesn't receive the ball, 1 continues through to the left corner, as player 2 reverses to 4. Player 5 screens for 3, who comes to the top (diagram 2). Player 4 reverses the ball to 3, who passes to player 5, who look for 1 in the corner. Player 1 catches the pass looking to shoot, drive (Iso) or pass to player 4 cutting down the lane or skip pass to player 2, cutting down to the right corner (diagram 3).

- Player 1 catches the pass in triple threat position, so Iso can be effective.
- Players 4 and 2 must cut hard to their respective areas, so they can keep the defense honest (diagram 3).

Wheel

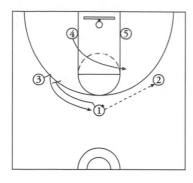

Diagram 1

Diagram 2

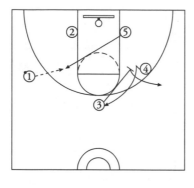

Diagram 3

Diagram 4

Purpose:

To execute an effective continuity motion offense that utilizes the flex cut, backscreens and screenthe screener options.

Organization:

"Wheel" begins in a 1-2-2 alignment with basic downscreens. Player 1 passes to 2 on the wing and sets an away screen for player 3 (diagram 1). Player 2 passes to 3, then makes a quick v-cut toward baseline to set up defender. Player 3 catches the pass from 2 and immediately reverses the bal to player 1, who has popped out to wing. Player 4 steps out to backscreen 2, who makes a hard cut to ball-side block or high post — if defended (diagram 2). As player 2 makes a "wheel" through the lane, player 5 should flash directly to open post (post not occupied by 2). Player 3 sets a screen 4, who comes to the top of key for screen-the-screener. Player 3 then fades to wing after screening for 4 (diagram 3). Player 1 starts reversal with pass to 4 and the wheel begins again (diagram 4).

Hot Tips

- Multi-purpose offense that exploits numerous scoring options for all 5 players.
- If player 2 did flash to high post instead of low block, then player 5 would cut to low block (diagram 3).

Hawk

Diagram 1

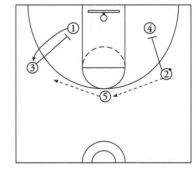

Diagram 2

Diagram 3

Diagram 4

Purpose:

To use single and double screens to create a high percentage shot opportunity.

Organization:

Player 4 downscreens for player 2. Player 2 passes to 2, then downscreens for player 5 on the opposite block. Player 5 replaces at the top of the key (diagram 1). Player 2 passes to 5, as player 3 downscreens for 1 on the left wing (diagram 2). Player 5 passes to 1, as player 2 starts to downscreen for player 4 (diagram 3). Players 2 and 5 then set the stagger double downscreen for player 4. Player 4 curls into the lane looking for a shot (diagram 4).

Variation:

After the doublescreen by players 5 and 2, player 5 could dive to the basket (diagram 4).

Hot Tips

• Wait for the screens.
• Read the defense.

Post Entry Movement

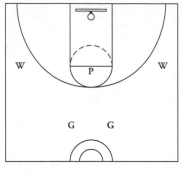

Diagram 1

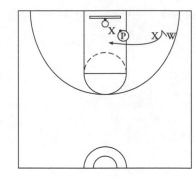

Diagram 2

Diagram 3

Diagram 4

Diagram 5

Diagram 6

Purpose:

To execute an effective man-man offensive set that provides opportunities to get ball to low post, while maintaining backdoor cutting options.

Organization:

In our regular man offense, we surround the high post with four players. These guards and wings will have to move and cut around the high post. The wings are located on the foul line extended near the sideline. The guards are located at the elbow extended near the ten second line (diagram 1). If the defender leaves to double down, the passer takes one step either to the left or right for the return pass. If the defender goes half way down to the post, the passer immediately cuts off the post looking for the handoff. If the defender stays, the passer immediately up-screens for the strong-side guard at the elbow. We then run a couple of options dependent upon the defenders (diagrams 2 and 3). We can have the guard curl to the hoop with the wing opening up for the jump shot (diagram 4). We can have the guard flare to the corner with the wing cutting hard to the hoop (diagram 5).

Variations:

- Diagrams 6 (cut off and curl) and 7 (flare): We try not to reverse the ball from the corner by passing it. This gives the defense a great angle for possibly stealing the ball. Whenever it is in the corner we try to bring the ball out by dribble. We dribble the ball out of the corner toward the wing. Any player in the wing position has to automatically cut to the hoop. If there is a player in the low post the cutter can now use the low post player to either, cut off and curl or flare to the corner.

- We can hit the cutter or the post. The dribble must reverse his pivot in order to hit the cutter if he goes to the corner. You can use this as a play by having the guard pass to the wing and cut to the corner, attempt a post entry, and then dribble-reverse the ball (diagrams 8, 9 and 10).

- We can create some possible backdoor action when the high post dives into the low post. The weak-side wing replaces the post by flashing into the high post for the pass from the wing. The high post player now has to face the hoop by using a drop pivot. High post can hit the low post who ducks-in, shoot the baby jumper, take it to the hoop opposite the low post, or hit the weak side guard who is going backdoor. The high post must use a reverse pivot in order create the proper space to see all these options (diagrams 11, 12 and 13).

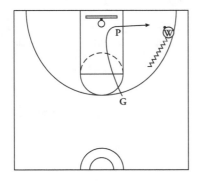

Diagram 7

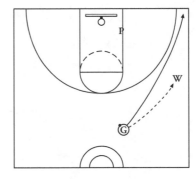

Diagram 8

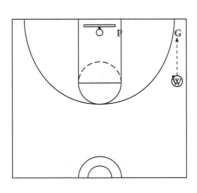

Diagram 9

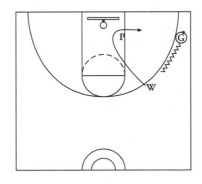

Diagram 10

Hot Tips

- Keep your players moving! By keeping the weak-side defenders occupied your create scoring opportunities.
- *Positions:* Guards and wings have to be able to handle the ball and shoot well. The more shooters you have out there the better this offense works. It helps if the post can shoot also. They need to pass well, shoot the ten-footer, and have some offensive capability in the low post.
- If the offense is working the low post will get opportunities to score. Without weak-side help we should be able to get the ball inside. Please note post entry is a skill that you might have to work on with your players. The time put in here is worthwhile. Obviously, the same can be said for low post moves.
- Our goal is to take away weak side defense (diagram 1).
- The movement of the player after making the entry pass is important (diagrams 2 and 3).
- Again, we breakdown these moves and drill them constantly. Proper footwork is always important (diagram 5).
- This is automatic whenever the ball is in the corner and the dribble is still alive. We call this "dribble reverse." (Diagrams 8, 9 and 10)

Diagram 11

Diagram 12

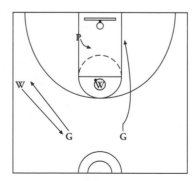

Diagram 13

Hubie

Diagram 1

Diagram 2

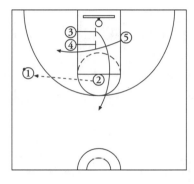

Diagram 3

Diagram 4

Purpose:

To execute a man-man offense, that initiates from a 1-4 high alignment and utilizes multiple screen-the-screener options; exploiting scoring options on the perimeter and in the low post.

Organization:

Player 1 passes to 2 on the right wing, receives a back screen from 5 and cuts to the low ballside block. As player 1 is cutting off of 5's backscreen, 3 and 4 cut down to the opposite block for a double screen (diagram 1). After a screen for 1, player 5 steps across to execute a pick and roll with 2. As players 5 and 2 execute the pick and roll on the right side, player 1 continues through, coming off a double screen from 3 and 4 to the left wing. Player 2 looks for 1 popping out to the left wing or 5 rolling to the right block (diagram 2). Player 1 looks to hit 5 in the low post or 3 popping out to the top (diagram 4).

Variation:

If player 2 passes to 1, player 5 receives a double cross screen from players 3 and 4 and posts up on the left block. Player 3 then releases from the double screen and receives a downscreen from player 2, and pops out to the top of key (diagram 3).

Player 2 must come off of 5's pick and roll and get to the middle of the free throw line to create enough space for a great passing angle to either player 1 who is popping out or player 5 who is rolling to the right block (diagram 2).

C-3

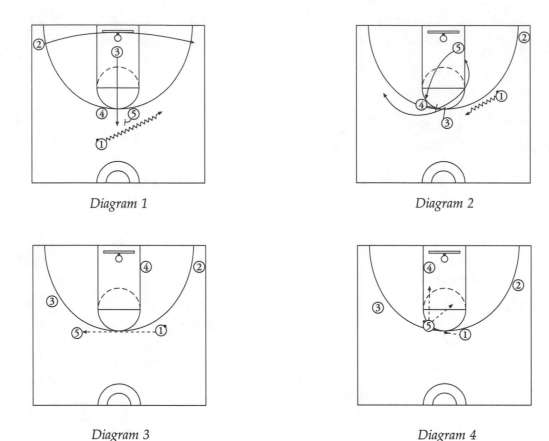

Diagram 1   Diagram 2

Diagram 3   Diagram 4

Purpose:

To execute an effective quick hitting man-man offensive play that culminates into a motion offense, and utilizes flare screens to exploits scoring options.

Organization:

Player 1 executes a pick and roll with 5 (who rolls to the basket). Player 1 dribbles off to the right wing. Player 3 cuts up the middle of the lane to the top. Player 2 cuts baseline from left corner to right corner (diagram 1). Player 4 turns and sets a flare screen at the top for 3, who cuts off to the left wing (behind the three-point line). Player 1 dribbles hard at screen and hits 3 (diagram 2) for either a three-point shot or a catch and drive on the clear out.

Variations:

- If player 3 is not open, 1 and 4 execute a pick and roll, as player 5 flashes to the high post (free throw line area). Player 1 looks for player 5 at the high post (diagram 3).

- Player 5 who can shoot the jump shot, drive or look to pass to 4, who had rolled to the basket (diagram 4).

- Player 1 can turn corner on pick and roll. Player 2 must wait to cut baseline to baseline (diagram 1).

- This continues into 4-out motion offense.

Kuemper

Diagram 1

Diagram 2

Diagram 3

Diagram 4

Diagram 5

Diagram 6

Purpose:

To execute an effective man-man continuity offense that utilizes a triangle scoring attack with a high post, low block and guard side threat.

Organization:

Player 1 passes 2 on the right wing and cuts in front to ballside corner. Player 4 flashes from left block to top of key (diagram 1). Player 2 reverses the ball to 4 (diagram 2). Player 4 reverses the ball to 3 on the

Diagram 7

Diagram 8

Diagram 9

left wing and then downscreens for 5 on the right block in the low post (diagram 3). Player 5 comes off of 4's downscreen to the top of key (high post). Player 4 flashes to ball-side block after screen for 5 (diagram 4). Player 3 reverses the ball to 5, as 5 immediately looks into 4, who has stepped over and sealed the defender. Simultaneously, players 1 and 2 interchange from wing to corner (diagram 5). Player 1 makes a backdoor cut from right wing, as 2 flashes up from right corner, replacing 1 (diagram 6). Player 5 reverses the ball to 2, as 1 continues his backdoor cut to opposite corner (diagram 7). Player 5 sets a down screen for 4 (diagram 8). Player 4 pops out to the top of key (high post) while 5 rolls back to ballside block. Player 2 passes to 5, looking to score (diagram 9).

Hot Tips

- Initial set up is as follows: player 1 is with ball at top, 2 is on the right wing, 3 is on the left wing, 4 is on the left block and 5 is on the right block.
- The top player (1) in the exchange must cut inside while the bottom player (2) cuts outside (diagram 5). This continuity is continued until you get the desired look.
- Post players must read the defense and can curl the screen, slip the screen or give and go.

Watervliet

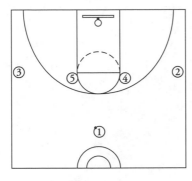

Diagram 1

Diagram 2

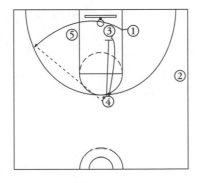

Diagram 3

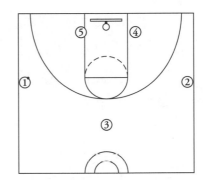

Diagram 4

Purpose:

To execute an effective quick hitter versus a man-to-man defense that is initiated out of a 1-4 high alignment and leads into 3-out, 2-in motion offense.

Organization:

Initial set up is as follows: Player 1 is at the top, players 2 and 3 are on the wings (right and left) and players 4 and 5 are on the elbows (diagram 1). Player 1 passes to player 2, cuts off a ballside high post screen from player 4 and goes to post up on ballside block. After the screen player 4 steps out and receives a return pass from player 2 and players 3 and 5 set a stagger double screen for player 1 on the opposite side (diagram 2). Player 1 either fades or pops out off the stagger double screen from players 3 and 5. Player 4 passes to player 1 then downscreens for player 3 (diagram 3).

Hot Tip   After the initial execution of the play, the players are in a 3-2 set and run motion (diagram 4).

Fist

Diagram 1

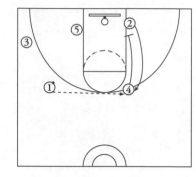

Diagram 2

Diagram 3

Diagram 4

Purpose:

To execute an effective man-man set play that exploits a perimeter and low post scoring option.

Organization:

Player 4 sets a ballscreen for 1, who dribbles to the left. At the same time, player 5 downscreens for 3, popping out to left wing (diagram 1). As player 1 dribble clears, player 4 downscreens for 2, who pops out to top of key (diagram 2). Player 1 passes to 2 for the open shot (diagram 3).

Variation:

If player 2 does not have an open look, 2 passes to player 4 in the low post for isolation (diagram 4).

Initial set up is as follows: player 1 is on the right sideline with the ball, 2 is on the right block, 3 is on the left block, 4 is right side (beyond 3-point line), and 5 is on the left wing.

Aquinas

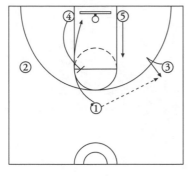

Diagram 1

Diagram 2

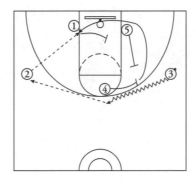

Diagram 3

Purpose:

To execute an effective man-man set play that utilizes a pick and roll into a double staggered screen to exploit a low post scoring opportunity.

Organization:

Players 4 and 5 flash up to high post (left and right elbows). Player 1 passes to player 3 on the right wing (diagram 1). Player 4 sets a back screen for 1, who cuts off to the left block. Player 5 cuts back down to right block (diagram 2). Player 4 sets a ballscreen (pick and roll) for 3. As player 3 uses the screen, (coming to the middle), player 4 cuts off double staggered backscreens from players 5 and 1, to the left block. Player 3 reverses the ball to 2 on the left wing, who passes to player 4 in the low post (diagram 3).

Hot Tips

- Initial set up is as follows: Player 1 is with ball at top, 2 is on the left wing, 3 is on the right wing, 4 is on the left block and 5 is on the right block.
- As soon as player 4 sets a ballscreen for 3, 4 must release and cut hard off of 5 and 1's screens (diagram 3).
- Player 3 must get to the middle of the free throw lane to create a good passing angle to 2, who can hit 4 posting (diagram 3).

Clear

Diagram 1

Diagram 2

Diagram 3

Purpose:

To execute a quick man-man set play that utilizes the 1-4 high alignment and exploits your best shooter.

Organization:

Player 1 passes to player 5 on the left elbow. Player 3 cuts back door, looking for the pass from player 5. If not open, player 3 flashes back to left wing (diagram 1). Player 2 cuts from the right wing and stops in the paint. Player 4 sets a backscreen for player 1, who fades to the wing for a shot or clear out, receiving the pass from player 5 (diagram 2). If player 1 doesn't shoot, then players 4 and 5 set a side by side double down screen for player 2, flashing up the middle (diagram 3).

Player 1 can dribble to either side to initiate the play.

Section Two:
Zone Offense

Lee U.

Diagram 1

Diagram 2

Diagram 3

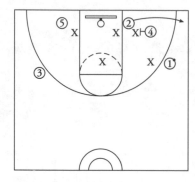

Diagram 4

Purpose:

To execute an effective quick hitter offense verses a 2-3-zone defense that utilizes player 2 as the best shooter.

Organization:

Player 1 passes to 2 on the right wing (diagram 1). Player 2 passes to 4 in the right corner and cuts to ballside block. Player 1 flashes to right wing, replacing 2 (diagram 2). Player 4 reverses the ball to 1 on the right wing and screens in for 2 (diagram 3). Player 2 pops out to right corner for 3-point shot, as 4 seals the defender (diagram 4).

- Initial set up is as follows: player 1 is with the ball at the top of the key (right lane side), player 2 is on right wing, player 4 is in right corner, player 3 is on the left wing and player 5 is in the left "short-corner" area.
- Player 2 is your best shooter and 4 can screen middle or low block zone defender (diagram 3).

Corner

Diagram 1

Diagram 2

Diagram 3

Diagram 4

Diagram 5

Diagram 6

Purpose:

To execute an effective continuity zone offense (with variations) that utilizes perimeter passing and cutting.

Organization:

Initial set up is with player 1 near the middle of the floor, player 5 in the high post, players 2 and 3 wing (where 3 is free throw line extended and 2 is in the corner by the baseline) and player 4 is out on perimeter (diagram 1). Player 1 hits the strong side by passing to player 4 and cuts down to ballside block area. Player 5 slides to toward ballside elbow, and player 3 rotates to top (diagram

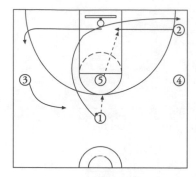

Diagram 7   *Diagram 8*

2). Player 4 can pass to player 2 in corner then make a banana cut to short corner or the corner. Player 1 cuts through on the pass and fills opposite wing. Player 2 drives up toward defense and should look to player 4 on the banana cut or player 5 in high post (diagram 3). If 2 passes to 5 in high post, then 4 dives baseline (diagram 4). If 2 passes to 4, then 5 dives middle (diagram 5).

Variations:

- Player 1 passes to player 3 on weak side wing, and then dives to block area, as player 5 slides to ballside. Player 2 cuts from right to left corner, (ensuring the left side is now strong). Player 4 rotates up to top (diagram 6).

- Player 3 now passes to player 2 in the corner and executes strong side rules, for example the banana cut to short corner or the corner (diagram 7).

- Player 1 passes to player 5 (high post). Player 5 catches, and immediately faces the basket and looks for player 2 cutting. Player 1 dives middle toward weak side and, then cuts right baseline filling player 2's spot. Player 3 rotates to the top. After cutting, player 2 can go through to opposite wing (diagram 8).

Hot Tips

- Note, player 4's banana cut should be to block/rim area.
- Player 1 should look for ball on opposite block as well (diagram 3).
- Be patient, lay-ups can be had in this offense.
- Player 1 should look for ball on opposite block as well (diagram 3).
- Try to work the ball inside, forcing the defense to decide on whom to cover.
- Don't be afraid to pass to the cutters if they are open.
- As offense runs through, players 1, 2, 3 and 4 will rotate five spots. Here are the rules to follow:
  a) If pass comes down from the middle, cut to block and go through on next pass.
  b) If you pass from the wing, banana cut and go back to baseline.

St. John's

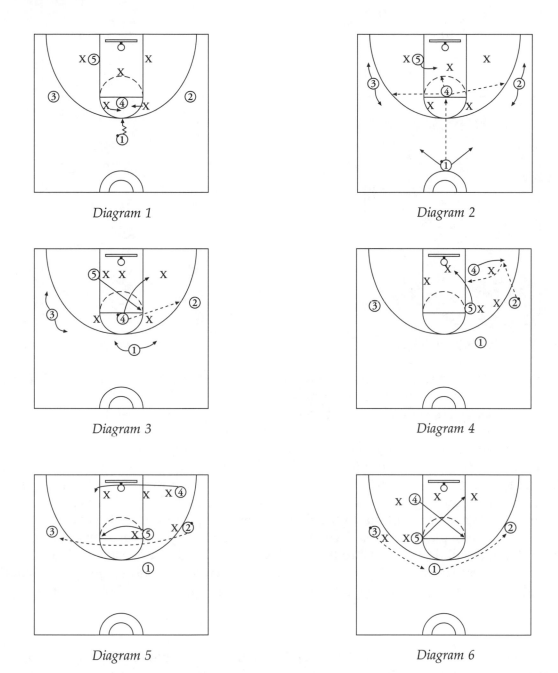

Diagram 1

Diagram 2

Diagram 3

Diagram 4

Diagram 5

Diagram 6

Purpose:

To execute an effective zone offense verses a 2-3 zone defense with a 1-3-1 alignment.

Organization:

We use an odd front against an even front zone. Players 1, 2 and 3 are perimeter players. Player 1 is at the point position, 2 and 3 are on the wings. Players 4 and 5 are the post players. Players 1, 2 and 3 work with each other, and 4 and 5 work together. Perimeter players will gap the zone. Players 2 and 3 should be between the front and back of the zone. Player 1 needs to attack the gaps

Diagram 7

Diagram 8

Diagram 9

Diagram 10

with his dribble. When he can draw the defenders in he should kick the ball. Player 4 is at the free throw line and 5 is on one of the blocks (diagram 1).

If player 4 receives a pass from player 1, 4 will have the following options: Player 4 can pass to player 2 or 3 spotting-up, 4 can pass to player 5 who is ducking-in strong, 4 can pass back to 1 who then will move to an open area (diagram 2). On any pass to the wing, player 2 or 3, both post players will X cut to the ballside. In this case, player 5 will flash to the elbow and 4 will cut to the block. When player 2 receives the ball he has the following options: 2 can hit either post player with a pass, 2 can pass to 1 at the top of the key, or 2 can skip pass to 3 who has moved to an open area (diagram 3). Player 4 can step-out to the short corner after posting-up. If player 2 hits 4 in the short corner with a pass, player 5 must dive to the rim (diagram 4). If player 2 hits 3 with a skip pass, players 4 and 5 will flash directly to the ball, i.e., 4 goes to ballside block and 5 goes to ballside elbow (diagram 5). On ball reversal, post men will always x-cut to the ball when it arrives at the wing. On ball reversal, the wing and point will exchange positions when it arrives at the opposite wing (diagram 6).

Variations:

• Option Exchange: Player 1 passes to 2. Player 4, who dove to the block previously, steps-out to the short corner. Player 2 passes to 4 and then cuts to ballside block. Player 5, at foul line, now steps to the ballside elbow. Player 1 replaces 2 at the wing. Player 3 remains in the opposite wing area (diagram 7). Player 4 passes to 1, and then screens down on the bottom of the zone for 2. Player 1 fakes reversal and passes back to corner to 2, who has used 4's screen and went to the corner. 4 posts-up in the block. 3 is at the top of the key (diagram 8). Player 2 passes to 1. Player 1 reverses the ball to 3. Player 3 dribbles to the opposite wing. Both big men x-cut: player 5 dives to ball side corner and 4 flashes to ball side elbow. Player 1 replaces 3 at the top of the key. Player 2 can fill 1's spot or we can run exchange on the left side. If we run exchange, player 5 would step to corner and 2 would cut to the ball side box (diagram 9).

Diagram 11

Diagram 12

Diagram 13

Diagram 14

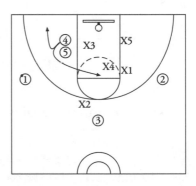

Diagram 15

- Option Fade: Player 1 passes to 2. Player 3 cuts ball side (it must be a hard cut to draw defensive attention). Player 2 passes to 3. Player 2 must look hard at 3 to sell the play (diagram 10). Player 1 cuts to opposite wing. Player 5 "X opposite" goes to weak side elbow and 4 goes to weak side block. Players 4 and 5 will screen the zone. Player 2 looks to skip pass to 1. Players 4 and 5 post-up after screening (diagram 11). If the zone cheats post-men will let them slip by their screens and then flash to the ball. Player 2 can hit either post-player with a pass (diagram 12).

- Option Stack: Player 1 (in this case, a shooter) passes to 2. Player 1 shallow cuts to 3. Player 3 replaces 1. Post players stack low opposite the ball (diagram 13). Player 3 receives a pass from 2 on the ball reversal. Player 3 dribbles at defensive guard (X2) then passes to 1. Players 4 and 5 screen bottom of zone. Player 1 looks for the jump shot (diagram 14). If wing defender (X3) successfully closes out on 1, player 5 will screen the interior of the zone (X4). Player 4 will curl cut over the top or goes to the short corner. Player 5 reads 4 and goes opposite. Player 1 looks to 4 or 5 (diagram 15).

Hot Tip   Initial set up is the odd front attack 1-3-1: player 1 has the ball at the top of the key, player 4 is at middle free throw line, player 2 is on the right wing, player 3 is on the left wing and player 5 is on the left block.

Patriot: Double Through-Out

Diagram 1

Diagram 2

Diagram 3

Diagram 4

Purpose:

To create a scoring opportunity against a zone defense by utilizing screens and exploiting the jump shot.

Organization:

Player 1 passes to player 5, who stepped out from the ballside high post. On the pass from player 1 to 5, player 3 cuts from the right wing, through the lane, to the left wing. Immediately, player 1 cuts high (right) side off player 5 and continues on to the weakside corner (diagram 1). Player 5 reverses the ball to player 2, who immediately reverses to player 3 on the left wing. Player 5 then dives to ballside (left) block. If player 3's defender closes-out, then the ball is passed to player 1 for a jump shot in the corner (diagram 2).

Variations:

- If player 1 has no shot, then 1 reverses the ball back to player 3, who immediately reverses it to player 2. Player 4 flashes from right post to free throw line area (diagram 3).

- Player 3 down screens the same ballside defender for player 1, who cuts to up to left wing. Player 5 steps in the lane reading defender. Player 2 passes to the open man (diagram 4).

Hot Tips

- Set solid screens on the zone defenders.

Patriot Action

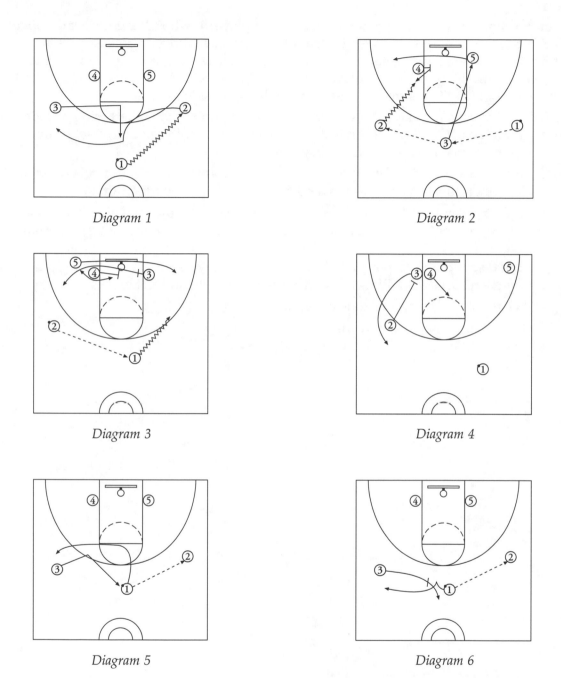

Diagram 1

Diagram 2

Diagram 3

Diagram 4

Diagram 5

Diagram 6

Purpose:

To create a scoring opportunity against a zone defense by utilizing screens and the dribble drive.

Organization:

Player 1 dribbles right toward player 2 on the right wing. Player 2 immediately makes a shallow cut to the top of the key and then flares to the left wing, replacing player 3. Player 3 flashes to the middle of the free throw line high post, and then pops out to the top of the key (diagram 1).

Player 1 reverses the ball to player 3, who reverses to player 2 on the left wing. Player 3 then cuts to the right block and player 2 attacks the basket with a dribble drive toward the left low post. Player 4 immediately cuts into the lane to set a cross screen for player 5. Player 5 cuts to the baseline and looks for a pass from player 2 (diagram 2).

Variations:

- If player 2 has no pass to player 5, then 2 reverses to player 1, who filled the vacant top after player 3 cut to the right block. Player 1 attacks the right side with a dribble drive. On the drive, player 5 runs from the baseline to the opposite (right) side coming off a stagger-double screen from player 4 (middle of lane) and player 3 (on the right block). After the screen, player 4 ducks in the lane and player 3 cuts from the baseline to the weak side (diagram 3).

- Player 2 down screens for player 3, who either comes to pop out to the left wing or fades to the left corner for a shot. Or, player 2 can just stay on left wing and receive reversal from player 1. Player 1 passes to open player: 3, 4 or 5 (diagram 4).

- Inside Cut Entry: Same as diagram 1, except player 1 passes to player 2 and cuts down to the free throw line and then fills left wing, as player 3 flashes to top of key (diagram 5).

- Flare Screen Entry: Same as diagram 1, except player 1 passes to player 2 and receives a flare, a back screen from player 3 and flares to left wing, as player 3 pops to top of key (diagram 6).

- Initial set up is with player 1 at the top of key, players 2 and 3 on the right and left wings, respectively. Players 5 and 4 are on the right and left blocks.
- Set solid screens on the zone defenders.
- Make hard cuts off of screens.

Delaware

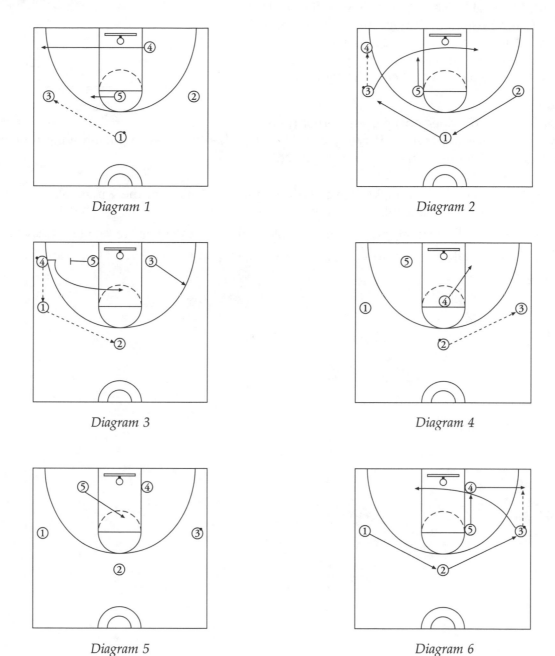

Diagram 1

Diagram 2

Diagram 3

Diagram 4

Diagram 5

Diagram 6

Purpose:

To execute an effective continuity half-court zone offense that utilizes cuts from the perimeter players and high/low flashes from the post players.

Organization:

Player 1 passes to player 3 on the left wing. Player 4 flashes from the right block to left corner. Player 5 goes from middle free throw line to ballside (left) elbow (diagram 1). Player 3 passes to player 4 and cuts through the middle of the zone, as player 5 flashes down to the ballside block.

Player 1 flashes to left wing and player 2 fills the top (diagram 2). Player 4 reverses the ball to player 1, receives a back screen from player 5 and flashes middle to high post (free throw line). Player 1 reverses to 2 (diagram 3). Player 2 reverses to player 3, as player 4 dives to right block (diagram 4). Player 3 looks to player 5, who flashes from left block to high post elbow (diagram 5). Start the rotation again: player 1 reverses to player 2, 2 passes to player 3, player 4 cuts to corner and receives the pass from 3, player 5 flashes to ballside block and 3 cuts through (diagram 6).

Diagram 7

Variations:

If player 3 cannot (or does not) pass to corner (player 4), then player 3 reverses to player 1. Player 1 calls "Rotate," then dribbles to the left wing replacing player 3, as 3 cuts through. The offense is restarted!

- Initial set is 1-3-1 attack! Player 1 at top, players 2 and 3 at the wings, player 5 at the free throw line and player 4 right on the block.
- On the ball reversal, player 1 must look at player 5 then pass to player 2 (diagram 3).
- Player 2 takes a hard look at player 5 and then passes to player 3 (diagram 4).

Virginia

Diagram 1

Diagram 3

Diagram 4

Purpose:

To execute an effective 1-4 high, half-court zone offense that utilizes screens from the post players and skip passes from the stationary perimeter players.

Organization:

Player 1 dribbles off a high post screen from player 5. Player 2 cuts down from wing to corner (diagram 1). As player 1 dribbles below the free throw line and passes to player 2 in the corner, player 4 cuts from weakside elbow and sets a ball screen for player 3 (diagram 2). Player 2 skip passes to player 3, as player 1 flashes back to the top. Player 5 cuts down to weakside block to prepare for screen (diagram 3).

Variation:

If player 3 has no shot, then 3 skips the ball to player 2 for a shot. Player 4 and 5 backscreen the zone defender.

- Skip passes as often as possible.
- Post players must cut and screen hard.

Oklahoma

Diagram 1

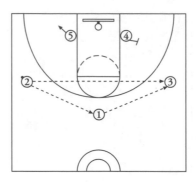

Diagram 2

Diagram 3

Diagram 4

Purpose:

To execute an effective half-court zone offense.

Organization:

Player 2 dribbles to the left wing as player 1 pops to the top and player 3 fades to the opposite wing. Player 5 posts up on left block and player 4 steps in for rebounding position on weak-side (diagram 1). Player 2 skip passes to player 3 or reverses to player 1 to pass to 3. Player 4 posts up on right block and player 5 steps back off left block (diagram 2). Player 2 screens the wing defender, while player 1 flashes to left wing for a "skip pass" jumper. Player 5 backscreens the back defender, then posts up. Player 4 positions for weakside rebound. Player 3 skip passes to 1 (diagram 3).

Variation:

If player 1 does not shoot, then 1 can penetrate the zone, as player 2 screened and filled the top and player 3 faded to the corner (diagram 4).

- Set good backscreens.
- Make good skip passes.

2-1-2 Cross Over

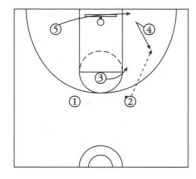

Diagram 1

Diagram 2

Diagram 3

Diagram 4

Purpose:

To execute an effective zone offense out of a 2-1-2 set that utilizes baseline cuts and high/low post flashes.

Organization:

Start in a 2-1-2 set up. Player 2 passes the ball to player 4 after cut. Player 5 flashes behind the zone, cutting behind the backboard. Player 3 cuts from middle free throw line to high post ballside elbow (diagram 1). Player 1 cuts down to weak side for rebounding. Player 4 has three options: hit player 5 in the block area after cross over, pass to player 3 at elbow, or reverse back to player 2 at top (diagram 2). If player 4 passes to the player 5, then 5 can shoot, hit player 3 cutting to basket, pass to player 1 on opposite baseline or reverse to player 4 (diagram 3).

Variation:

If player 5 passes to player 4, then 4 reverses to player 2, as player 1 breaks out to receive pass from 2. Player 3 flashes from middle free throw line to left block. Player 5 flashes from short corner to the free throw line, replacing player 3 (diagram 4).

In diagram 4 the crossover can be restarted.

Regular

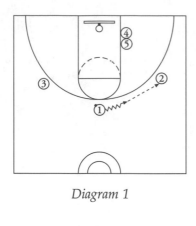

Diagram 1

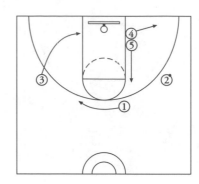

Diagram 2

Diagram 3

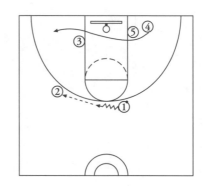

Diagram 4

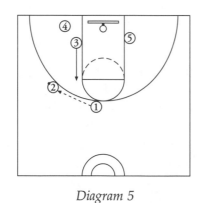

Diagram 5

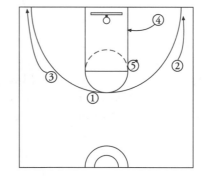

Diagram 6

Purpose:

To execute a continuity zone offense that is initiated from a stack alignment and then utilizes an effective 3-out-2-in motion concept.

Organization:

Player 1 takes the ball to the side of the stack (right) to run this play and passes to player 2 (diagram 1). As soon as player 2 receives the pass, players 5 and 4 pop the stack, to the high right elbow

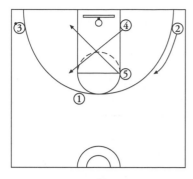

Diagram 7

Diagram 8

and right sort corner, respectively. Player 1 relocates to the left side of the key as player 3 spots up on the weak side wing (diagram 2). Player 2 tries to hit player 4, stepping out to the short. If player 4 receives the pass, then player 3 moves to the opposite block and screens for player 2 as the cut is made to the basket and continued to the left wing. Player 5 cuts to the ballside block, trailing player 2's cut. Player 1 flashes to ballside of key (diagram 3). The action is repeated on the opposite (left) side of the floor as player 1 passes to player 2 (diagram 4). On the pass from player 1 to 2, player 4 cuts from right short corner to left short corner, as player 3 flashes from low left block to high post (diagram 5). The offense now shifts into a 3-out-2 zone offense with the 4 and 5 crossing the paint on the pass (diagram 6, 7, 8) looking for high-low action and skip passes.

Variations:

• If player 2 or 5 is not successful in receiving the pass from player 4, and then the ball is reversed to player 1 at the top of key (diagram 3).

• When player 5 receives the ball in the high post, player 4 immediately ducks in from short corner to low post, looking for the pass. Player 3 relocates to the weak-side corner, as player 2 fills ballside corner (diagram 6).

• Player 5 hits player 3 in the left corner and then flashes hard to ballside block. Player 4 immediately cuts hard from right block to left elbow (diagram 7).

Hot Tips

• Stack alignment can create match-up problems for the zone.

• The "X" movement from players 5 and 4 can be a devastating high/low option.

• In the 3-out-2 in zone offense, players 4 and 5 try to create high/low opportunities with every pass.

Regular 2

Diagram 1

Diagram 2

Diagram 3

Diagram 4

Purpose:

To execute a continuity zone offense that is initi-ated from a stack alignment and then utilizes an effective 3 out 2-motion concept.

Organization:

Player 1 takes the ball away from the stack and passes to player 3 on the left wing. On the pass, player 2 immediately cuts below the stack to the left short corner looking for the pass (diagram 1). If player 2 receives the ball, player 5 flashes to the high post (left elbow) and player 4 flashes to ballside block looking for a bounce pass from player 2 or high/low pass from 5 (diagram 2).

Diagram 5

Variations:

- If player 2 is not open, then player 3 reverses the ball to player 1 and cuts baseline below the stack screen to the right wing (diagram 3).
- As player 2 is cutting baseline to the right wing, player 3 is following the cut and going off the stack screen to the right corner (diagram 4).

- The zone is distorted when player 2 receives the pass and attacks the right elbow, as player 3 fills the corner for the open look (diagram 5).

- Players 4 and 5 set a stack screen against the baseline of the zone (diagram 3).
- When player 3 receives the pass, players 5 and 4 pop the stack once again, looking for the high/low (diagram 5).

Quick Lob

Diagram 1

Diagram 2

Purpose:

To execute a quick scoring opportunity versus a 2-3 zone defense.

Organization:

Player 1 dribbles hard toward left wing and makes the pass to player 3 in the mid-wing area (diagram 1). Player 5 sprints along the right baseline as player 3 passes back out to 1. As player 1 begins dribbles, player 3 takes two steps following 1. Player 4 flashes into middle of paint to occupy the defense. As player 4 flashes, player 5 sets a blindside backscreen on the defensive player guarding 3. Player 3 makes a hard cut to the basket looking for the lob (diagram 2).

Variations:

Player 1 can deliver the lob or reverse the ball to player 2 on the opposite side to deliver it.

- Make the defense come out and guard the wing player. This can occur by having player 3 catch the ball in between the corner and wing areas. If the guard defends the wing, this play won't work.
- Player 3 keeps acting like he wants the ball after passing it back to player 1.

Drive

Diagram 1

Diagram 2

Diagram 3

Purpose:

To execute and utilize screening as an effective quick hitter verses a 2-3 zone defense.

Organization:

Player 5 starts behind the weak side defender. Player 4 starts on the right block. Player 1 passes to player 2 (diagram 1). Player 2 catches the ball from player 1 and drives to the baseline attempting to draw the baseline defender. Player 4 screens the middle of the zone for player 5, who flashes to right post area (diagram 2).

Variation:

If player 2 is successful in pulling out the defender, 2 will pass to player 5 coming off the screen from player 4 for lay-up. If the baseline defender stays, player 2 can pull up for a short jump shot (diagram 3).

Player 2 is your best midrange shooter (diagram 1).

Screen

Diagram 1

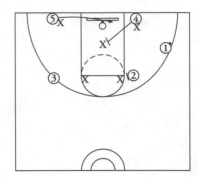

Diagram 2

Diagram 3

Purpose:

To execute and utilize screening as an effective quick hitter verses a 2-3 zone defense.

Organization:

Player 5 starts behind the weak-side defender. Player 4 starts on the right block. Player 2 screens the top defender for player 1 (diagram 1). As player 1 comes off the screen from player 2, attempting to draw the baseline defender. Player 4 screens the middle of the zone for player 5, who flashes to right post area (diagram 2).

Variation:

If player 1 is successful in pulling out the defender, 1 will pass to player 5 coming off the screen frm player 4 for a lay-up. If the baseline defender stays, player 1 can pull up for a short jump shot (diagram 3).

You may want to start the play with player 3 having the ball. As the ball is moved from player 3 to 1, the zone reacts and it is easier for player 2 to set the screen.

Double Hedge

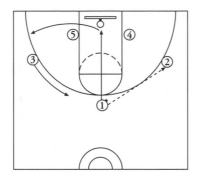

Diagram 1

Diagram 2

Diagram 3

Diagram 4

Purpose:

To execute a continuity zone offense that utilizes cuts from the perimeter players (wing to corner and corner to wing) and post players (flashing from opposite block) to ballside elbow.

Organization:

Player 1 passes the ball to player 2 on the right wing, and cuts down the middle of the lane. Player 3 flashes up to the top of the key to fill the spot of player 1 (diagram 1). Player 2 dribbles toward player 3, makes the pass and then cuts to opposite corner (left). Player 3 catches the pass from player 2 and then reverses to player 1. Player 4 flashes from right block to high post, left elbow (diagram 2). Player 2 reverses back to player 1 and cuts back to right wing. Player 1 reverses back to player 3 and cuts opposite to right corner. Player 4 dives to ballside block (diagram 3). Player 3 passes to player 2, who passes to player 1 in the right corner. Player 5 flashes from left block to high post, right elbow (diagram 4).

Hot Tips

- Wing and corner players reverse the ball to the top and cut to opposite wing or corner.
- On any reversal, opposite block post players flash to ballside elbow and ballside dive high post to elbow to ballside block.

Bomber

Diagram 1

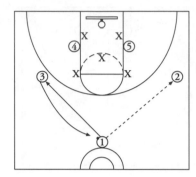

Diagram 2

Diagram 3

Diagram 4

Purpose:

To effectively execute a zone offense verses a 2-3 zone.

Organization:

Initial set up is with player 1 starting with the ball up top, players 5 and 2 on the left block in a stack, and players 4 and 3 in a stack on the left side (diagram 1). Players 2 and 3 pop out to free throw line extended on their respective sides (right and left). Player 1 passes to 2 (diagram 2). After the pass is made from player 1 to player 2, 1 interchanges with player 3, player 4 flashes to high post (ballside) elbow, and player 5 steps out into the short corner

Diagram 5

(diagram 3). Player 2 passes to player 3, 3 immediately reverses it to player 1 on left wing (diagram 4). Player 2 backscreens player 3 for a flare to the right wing. Simultaneously, player 4 downscreens for player 5, who cuts off the screen to the high post (ballside elbow) looking for pass from player 1 (diagram 5).

Variation:

If player 5 cannot receive the pass from player 1, 5 will step out and set a screen for 1, initiating the penetrate and pitch.

Minutemen

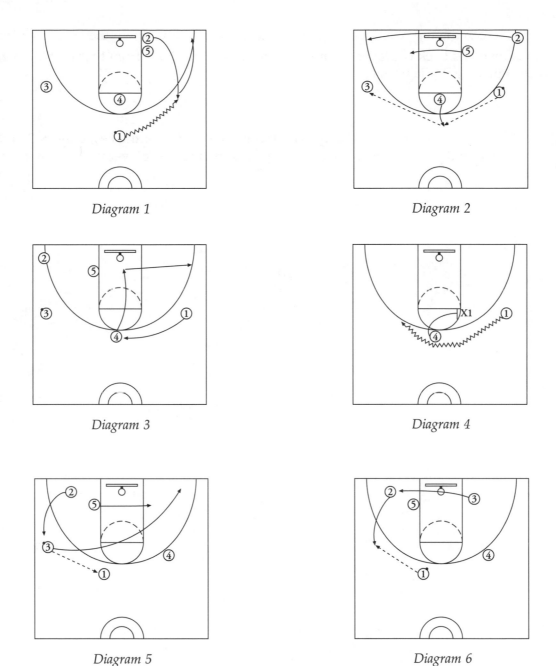

Diagram 1

Diagram 2

Diagram 3

Diagram 4

Diagram 5

Diagram 6

Purpose:

To effectively execute a zone offense that utilizes wing cuts and cut/replace action.

Organization:

Player 1 dribbles to the right wing, as player 2 flashes from the right block to the right wing and cuts to the ballside corner (diagram 1). Player 1 gets to the right wing and reverses to player 4 (who has popped out to the top of the key from the freethrow line) and reverses to player 3 on the left wing. Player 2 cuts from the right corner to the left corner. Player 5 flashes from the right block to the left block (diagram 2). Player 3 has the ball on the left wing, as player 4 cuts down the middle and to the right corner. Player 1 flashes to the top (diagram 3). Player 3 reverses the ball back to player 1, and if player 5 has his defender sealed, 5 flashes to the opposite block first and then to player 3 after a pass to player 1 (diagram 5).

Variations:

- Player 4 can screen the top defender for player 1, instead of cutting down the lane (diagram 4).
- If the ball is reversed back to player 2 from 1, player 3 now cuts back from the right block to the left corner, replacing 2 (diagram 6).

 Initial set up is as follows: player 1 attacks from the top of the key, players 2 and 5 are stacked on the right block, player 3 is on the left wing and player is at the free throw line.

Tech/Stagg

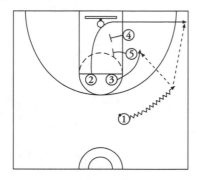

Diagram 1

Diagram 2

Diagram 3

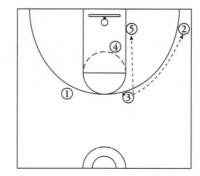

Diagram 4

Purpose:

To execute an effective zone offense that utilizes screens to exploit multiple low post and perimeter scoring options.

Organization:

Player 1 dribbles to right wing, as 2 cuts from free throw line to right corner. Simultaneously, players 4 and 5 screen in on the zone defenders and 3 cuts down the middle right side (diagram 1). Player 1 looks for 2 in the right corner for a shot or 3 cutting down the lane for a lay-up (diagram 2).

Variations:

- Instead of player 1 dribbling to the right, 1 dribbles to the left and makes a reversal pass to 3, who has popped out from free throw line. Player 2 makes the same cut to the right corner, as 4 backscreens the middle defender of the zone for 5, who cuts to the hoop (diagram 3).

- Player 3 can make a quick post entry pass to 5 or reverse the ball to 2 for a shot in the corner (diagram 4).

Option: If player 2 does not have a quick shot, 2 immediately passes to 5, who has sealed the back zone defender (diagram 4).

Paul Culpo
Hartwick College

Zone-O

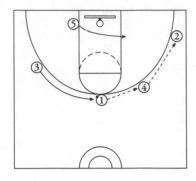

Diagram 1

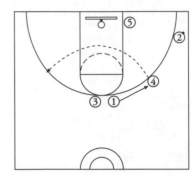

Diagram 2

Diagram 3

Diagram 4

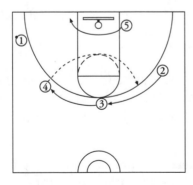

Diagram 5

Diagram 6

Purpose:

To execute an effective quick hitting zone offensive play that culminates into a continuity offense, and utilizes a designated perimeter player who makes shallow cuts through the zone, exploiting numerous scoring options.

Organization:

Player 1 passes to 4, who immediately passes to player 2 in the right corner. Player 5 cuts from left block to ballside short corner area, looking for pass from 2. Player 3 cuts from left wing to top (diagram 1). Player 4 makes a shallow cut through the zone, looking for pass from 2 or 5 (if 2 passes to 5) and continues through to the left wing. As player 4 cuts, 1 fills the right wing, replacing 4 (diagram 2).

Variations:

- If player 2 cannot pass to 5 or 4; the ball is reversed to 1. Player 1 passes to player 3, then 1 shallow cuts from right wing to left corner. Player 2 follows pass and replaces 1 on the right wing (diagram 3).

- Player 3 reverses the ball to 4 on the left wing, who passes to 1 in the ballside corner. Player 5 cuts from right block to ballside short corner area, looking for pass from 1 (diagram 4).

- Player 4 makes a shallow cut through the zone, looking for pass from 1, or 5 (if 1 passes to 5) and continues through to the left wing. As player 4 cuts, 3 fills the right wing, replacing 4 and 2 replaces 3 at the top (diagram 5).

- Player 1 reverses the ball to 3, then to 2, as 3 cuts to opposite corner. Player 1 fills 3's spot on the left wing (diagram 6).

- Initial set up is as follows: player 1 at the top with ball, 4 (is the "Rover") and on the right wing, 2 is right corner, 3 is left wing and 5 is left block.
- Player 4, Rover, is the best shooter, and the ball is swung through player 4 to the corner on all shallow cuts (diagram 1).
- Player 5 should work on catching and pivoting toward the baseline for post moves.
- Weakside players (1, 2 or 3 in the diagrams) should spot up on opposite elbow area when 5 catches the ball.
- This continuity stretches the zone, creates great looks and gets penetration opportunities.

Cougar

Diagram 1

Diagram 2

Diagram 3

Diagram 4

Purpose:

To execute an effective zone continuity offense verses a 1-3-1 defense that utilizes a perimeter and post scoring attack.

Organization:

Player 1 passes the ball to player 2 on the right wing. Player 5 cuts from ballside block to short corner. Player 4 moves from left block to mid-post area, sealing off the weakside wing defender (diagram 1). Player 1 steps back to receive reversal pass from 2 (diagram 2). Player 1 reverses the ball to 3, as player 4 now steps to the left short corner, while player 5 moves from to opposite short corner to mid-post area, sealing off the weakside wing defender (diagram 3). Player 3 passes to 5, cutting to basket after releasing from defender (diagram 4).

Hot Tips

- Initial set up is as follows: player 1 has the ball at the top of the key, 2 is on the right wing, 3 is on the left wing, 4 is on the left block and 5 is on the right block.
- Player 1 must attack the top defender with a strong dribble, to gain a better passing angle to 2 (diagram 1).
- The post players (4 and 5) must go get the opposite wing defender so they can back screen and seal (diagrams 1 and 3).
- The offensive concept is to allow the zone to shift and throw passes over the top. The more area the bottom has to cover the less effective the zone becomes.

Push

Diagram 1

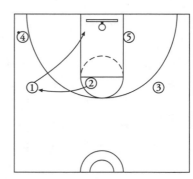

Diagram 2

Diagram 3

Diagram 4

Purpose:

To execute an effective zone offensive play that utilizes a perimeter and post scoring option.

Organization:

Player 1 passes to 4, who pops out from low post to the corner (diagram 1). Player 1 cuts to replace 4 at low block, as 2 flashes from free throw to left wing, replacing 1 (diagram 2). Player 4 reverses the ball to 2 and screens in for 1 (diagram 3). Player 2 has multiple options (diagram 4):

- Option-1 – pass to 1 in the corner for a shot.
- Option-2 – pass to 4 opening up after screen.
- Option-3 – pass to 5, flashing from right block to high post.

Initial set up is as follows: player 1 is on the left wing with the ball, 2 is in the high post at the free throw line, player 3 is on the right wing, 4 is on the left block, and 5 is on the right block.

Chicago

Diagram 1

Purpose:

To execute an effective zone offense quick hitter that initiates out of a 1-3-1 alignment and utilizes screening, cutting and ball reversal to exploit a scoring opportunity for both the point guard and post player.

Organization:

Player 1 passes to 4 on the right wing, cuts through the ballside of the zone and looks for the return pass from 4 for a lay-up and continues through to the short corner on the left side, receiving a screen from 5. Simultaneously, player 3 steps out from the free throw line to receive a reversal pass from 4. Player 3 immediately reverses the ball to 2 on the left wing, who can:

- Pass to 5 in the low post for a score.
- Pass to 1 in the short corner for a shot or a quick pass to 5 posting (diagram 1).

Hot Tips

- Initial set up is as follows: player 1 is with ball at top, 2 is on the left wing, 3 is at the free throw line, 4 is on the right wing and 5 is on the left block.
- Player 1 must cut hard through the zone and if 1 does not receive the return pass from 4, continue through, cutting under 5 to the short corner.
- Player 1 cutting under 5 forces the defense to guard to people.
- Can run the same play for high post player.

Jessica Mannetti
Greeens Farms Academy

Missouri Dragon

Diagram 1

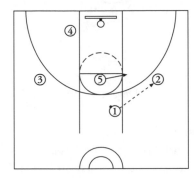

Diagram 2

Diagram 3

Diagram 4

Diagram 5

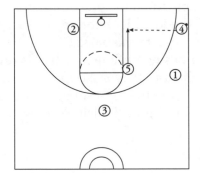

Diagram 6

Purpose:

To execute an effective zone offense that is useful against a 1-2-2, 2-1-2 and 2-3 zone defense. This offense is also highly effective against a man-to-man defense, utilizing cutters and exploiting the high/low post player isolation.

Diagram 7

Diagram 8

Organization:

Set up is as follows: player 1 has the ball at the top of the key, players 2 and 3 are on the right and left wings. Player 5 is in the middle of the free throw line, and player 4 is on the left block (diagram 1). Player 1 passes to player 2 on the wing (opposite of player 4). On the pass, player 5 flashes from the middle of the free throw line to ballside (right) elbow toward player 2 (diagram 2). After the pass to player 2, 1 cuts off of 5 at the high post to the basket looking for the give and go and continuing through to the left wing area if the pass is not received. Player 3 must flash to the top from the left wing to

Diagram 9

replace player 1 (diagram 3). After flashing to the top, player 3 makes an L-cut to the basket, running the defender off 5. Player 3 will look for a pass from player 2, continuing through if not open. Player 1 flashes to the top to replace player 3 (diagram 4). If player 1 and 3 are not open on the initial basket cuts, then player 4 flashes hard to the ballside (right) corner, thus creating two options for player 2 (diagram 5): pass to player 5 at the high post and execute a give and go backdoor cut to the basket or pass to player 4 in the corner and "face cut" the defender to the basket.

If player 4 cannot pass to player 2 cutting, then 2 must continue through to the opposite block as player 5 drops down from the high post creating two options (diagram 6): look for the pass from player 4 on the low block for an isolation move or step out on the baseline to set a backscreen so 4 can make a move to the basket.

If player 4 has no options, the ball is reversed to player 1 on the right wing, who reverses it to player 3 at the top. Player 2 pops out from the left block to the wing to receive the pass from player 3 (diagram 7). On the reversal pass from 3 to 2, player 5 makes a hard cut from the opposite, low block to the high-post (ballside) elbow. Player 2 looks to execute a give-n-go with player 5 (diagram 8).

Variation:

If you want to change the side of the floor that the offense is initiated from, then player 4 can back screen 3 or 5's defender with a fist symbol and roll to the basket on the cut. This creates two options for 1 depending on who's defender stays, player 1 can hit cutter with a pass or hit player 4 rolling to the basket (diagram 9).

Hot Tips

- Once player 2 has made a cut to the basket, players 3 and 1 must shift toward the ball to balance the floor (diagram 6).
- If player 5 is defended, then the offense is run off the left side of the floor (diagram 8).

Iowa

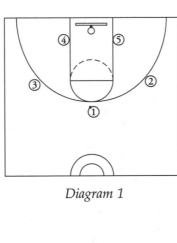

Diagram 1

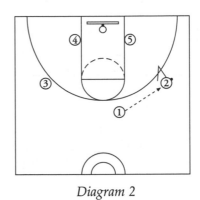

Diagram 2

Diagram 3

Diagram 4

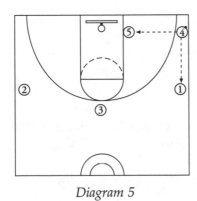

Diagram 5

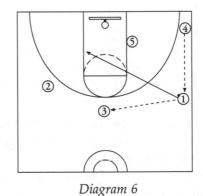

Diagram 6

Purpose:

  To execute an effective zone offense that is useful against a 1-2-2, 2-1-2 and 2-3 zone defense. This offense is also highly effective against a man-to-man defense, utilizing cutters and exploiting the high/low post player isolation.

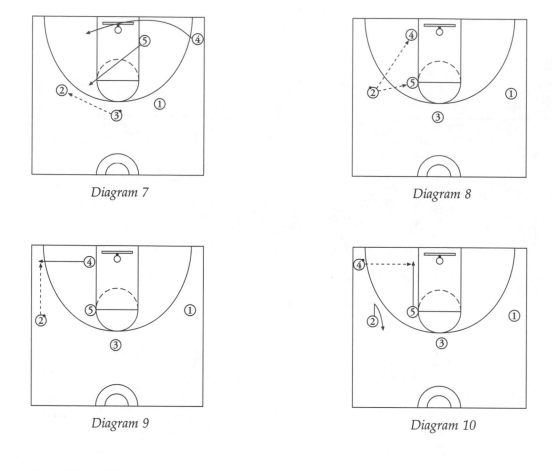

Diagram 7   Diagram 8

Diagram 9   Diagram 10

Diagram 11   Diagram 12

Organization:

Set up is as follows: player 1 has the ball at the top of the key, players 2 and 3 are on the right and left wings. Players 5 and 4 are on the right and left blocks (diagram 1). Player 2 v-cuts on the wing and receives a pass from player 1 — this is also the side that player 5 is posted on (diagram 2). Player 2 looks for player 5 in the low post, as player 4 times a cut from the left block to the ballside (right) corner (diagram 3).

Zone Overload — Player 2 passes to player 4 in the right corner and cuts through the middle, looking for the give and go and continuing through to the opposite wing/midcorner area (diagram 4). If player 2 did not receive the give and go pass, player 4 looks to drive baseline, pass to the post, or reverse the ball to player 1 (diagram 5). Player 1 catches the reversal pass from player 4 on the wing, looks for the dribble drive penetration or quick jump shot, before reversing it to player 3 at the top (diagram 6). Player 3 catches the pass at the top from player 1, and continues to reverse it to player 2 on the left wing. On the pass from player 3 to 2, player 5 cuts from right low block to ballside (left) high post elbow as player 4 cuts from right baseline corner to ballside (left) block (diagram 7). Player 2 looks to pass to player 5 in high post at ballside elbow or to player 4 in the low post area (diagram 8). If player 4 does not receive the ball from player 2 in the post, then player 4 must pop out to ballside corner looking for a quick pass and immediate shot or dribble-drive (diagram 9). On pass from player 2 to player 4, player 5 drops down from high post elbow to low block looking for the isolation. Player 2 v-cuts on the left wing to create a better passing angle for ball reversal (diagram 10).

Variation:

The positions in diagram 3 can actually be reversed (see diagram 11).

- Player 1 should always begin the play by dribbling to 1's side of the elbow high extended or the other side. This also helps to create a better passing angle from player 2 to player 5 in the post (diagram 1).
- Player 2 uses a bounce pass or "lob" pass to get player 5 the ball. Player 4 should do a self count of "three-one-thousand" before making the cut to the ballside corner (diagram 3).
- Players 1 and 3 must shift toward the ball, filling the open spots that are created by player 2's cut (diagram 4).
- If player 4 drives baseline, player 5 must create space by stepping toward the middle of the key, thus forcing the defender to follow. This will also allow player 4 to make a quick dish off to player 5 if the defender helps out (diagram 5).
- On any shot players 2 and 1 must drop down to rebound, players 5 must rebound from center of the lane, player 4 crashes the boards and rebounds on ballside and player 3 remains at top of key for defensive safety (diagram 12).

Section Three:
Out of bounds Plays

Man-Man Baseline: Texas

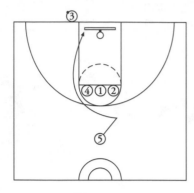

Diagram 1

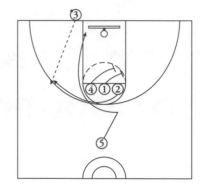

Diagram 2

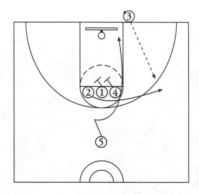

Diagram 3

Purpose:

To execute an effective baseline out of bounds play that utilizes the post player cutting to the basket for an initial scoring opportunity.

Organization:

Player 5 cuts from the top of the key to the ballside block looking to score off a pass from player 3 (diagram 1). After player 5 cuts off the left elbow, players 4 and 1 set a double screen for 2, who pops out to the left wing and looks for a pass from player 3 (diagram 2).

Variation:

The same play is run, but the ball is inbounded from the other side of the basket (diagram 3).

- Initial setup is as follows: Player 3 is the inbound passer, player 4 (ball side), player 1 (middle), and player 2 (opposite ball) line up side by side on the free throw line with player 5 at the top of the key, beyond the three-point line.
- Always look for player 5 on the intial cut to the basket.
- Player 4 is always ball side, 1 in the middle and 2 on the opposite ball side.
- Player 3 looks for player 2 popping out for a shot. If player 2 has no shot, 2 can look for 5, who turns and posts after the intial basket cut (diagram 2).

Man-Man Baseline: Automatic

Diagram 1

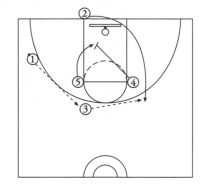

Diagram 2

Purpose:

To execute an effective baseline out of bounds play that utilizes your best shooter and post player.

Organization:

Player 1 v-cuts toward the middle of the lane and then slips between a double screen from players 3 and 5, cutting off to the ballside corner. After setting the screen for player 1, player 3 releases to top for a reversal pass while player 5 dives to ballside low post (diagram 1). After passing the ball to player 1, player 2 v-cuts off a down screen from player 4, looking for the pass from player 3 or skip pass from 1 player (if player 3 isn't open). Player 4 spins and seals inside, looking for a pass from 2. Player 5 also spins and seals, or flashes to middle of lane (diagram 2).

Variation:

Although the initial look is for player 2 to get a jump shot, a mismatch in the post will be created if the defense switches on player 4's screen (diagram 2).

Initial set up: Player 2 is the inbound passer, players 1, 3 and 5 are lined up ballside in this order and player 4 is opposite elbow.

Kendrick Saunders
Frostburg State University

Man-Man Baseline: Pick-the-Picker

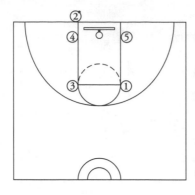

Diagram 1

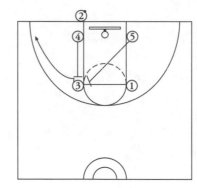

Diagram 2

Diagram 3

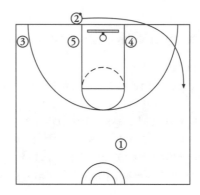

Diagram 4

Purpose:

To execute an effective baseline out of bounds that initiates from a box set and utilizes a screen the screenconcept to exploit scoring options.

Organization:

Players initiate from a box formation, with player 4 on the ballside block, 5 on opposite block, player 1 is diagonal from inbound passer on the opposite elbow, 3 is ballside elbow and 2 is in-bound passer (diagram 1). Player 4 turns and up screens for 3 (who fades to left short corner) on the ballside elbow. As player 4 reaches 3, 5 sets a diagonal screen for 4 (diagram 2). Player 4 uses back screen from 5 and dives to opposite block, looking for pass from 2. After a screen for player 4, 5 dives straight toward the ballside block. Player 1 fades back from opposite elbow for a defensive safety (diagram 3).

Variation:

After player 2 inbounds, 2 may then enter the court, cutting through to the right baseline (diagram 4).

Player 3 can fade to three-point area of left corner instead of short corner. Player 5 must start moving to screen 4 when 4 reaches the halfway point of lane. Basic Concept: Player 4 sets back screen and then receives a back screen.

Man-Man Baseline: Stack

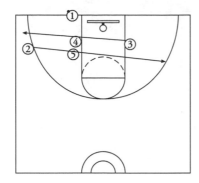

Diagram 1

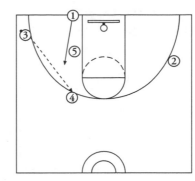

Diagram 2

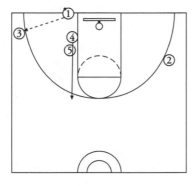

Diagram 3

Diagram 4

Purpose:

To execute an effective baseline out of bounds play that utilizes perimeter cutting and a ballside stack to free the inbound passer or post player for a score.

Organization:

Player 2 runs over the top of 4 and 5 in the ballside post to the opposite wing. Player 3 runs under the stack to get open in the corner (diagram 1). Player 1 passes the ball to 3 in the ballside (left) corner. Player 4 curls off of 5 in the stack and pops out to the ballside top (diagram 2). Player 3 reverses the ball to 4, as 1 begins to cut by 5 from out of bounds (diagram 3). Player 1 curls around 5 and cuts to opposite block. Player 5 reverse pivots and seals the defender, as 4 passes to 5 in the low post (diagram 4).

Variation:

Player 4 could actually pass to 1 curling around 5 in the midpost area for a jump shot (diagram 4).

- Initial set up is as follows: player 1 inbounds the ball, 4 and 5 are in a ballside block stack, 2 is ballside corner and 3 is opposite block.
- Player 2 cuts off the back end of 5, as 3 cuts off the front of 4 (diagram 1).
- Player 5 must stay facing player 1 when 1 comes from out of bounds, so 5 can then reverse pivot and seal (diagram 2).

Peter Wolf
Sante Fe Community College

Man-Man Baseline: Sante Fe

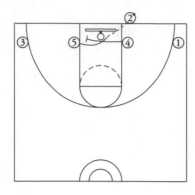

Diagram 1

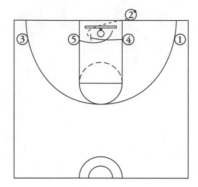

Diagram 2

Purpose:

To execute an effective baseline out of bounds play utilizing a 1-4 alignment with multiple options.

Organization:

- Option 1: Player 4 screens for 5. Player 2 looks to 5 for lob pass close to basket (diagram 1).

- Option 2: Player 4 screens for 5. If player 4's defender helps on 5, player 5 must reverse pivot to ball the defender behind. Player 2 passes to 4 (diagram 2).

- Option 3: Player 4 fakes screen and pops out to elbow. Player 1 screens 2 when coming from out of bounds. Player 4 passes to 2 for a three-point shot (diagram 3).

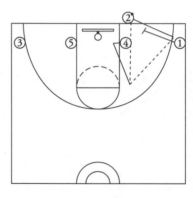

Diagram 3

Hot Tips

- Initial setup is as follows: Player 2 inbounds the ball, player 3 is wide out (opposite ball), player 5 is on the opposite block, player 4 is on the ballside block and player 1 is in the ballside corner.

- Players 1 and 3 have to stretch the defenders so they can't help (diagram 1).

138

Man-Man Baseline: Kings

Diagram 1

Diagram 2

Purpose:

To execute an effective baseline out of bounds play that utilizes your best shooter.

Organization:

Player 2 makes the inbounds pass to player 4, who has popped out to ballside wing off of the high elbow ballside stack. After receiving the pass, player 4 dribbles at 2 who has popped out to the right wing. Player 4 hands off the ball to player 2 and then sets a screen for 2. Player 2 looks for a jump shot (diagram 1).

Variation:

If player 2 has no initial shot after hand-off, then player 1 can backscreen player for 5, looking for a lob pass from 2. Player 2 can also pass to player 4 in the ballside corner, or reverse the ball to player 3 at the top of the key (diagram 2).

- Initial set is for player 2 the (best shooter) to inbound the ball. Players 1 and 4 are in a high stack on ballside elbow. Player 5 top of key and player 3 is on left wing.
- Player 4 rolls to ballside corner after hand-off to player 2 and player 3 flashes to top of key for defensive balance (diagram 2).
- Player 1 must wait to see if player 2 takes the shot and then back screen for player 5.

Man-Man Baseline: Screener

Diagram 1

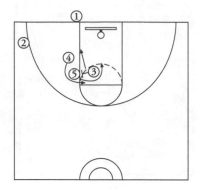

Diagram 2

Purpose:

To execute a baseline out of bounds play that utilizes numerous screens and flash cuts.

Organization:

Player 2 comes off a stagger double screen from players 4 and 5 and goes to the baseline corner. Player 3 comes to screen for player 5 (diagram 1). Player 5 curls to the middle off the pick from player 3, as player 4 rolls to the free throw line off the back pick immediately set by 3. If nothing is open, then player 3 flashes hard to ballside block (diagram 2).

Hot Tip   Player 1 is the inbound passer, as player 3 sets up opposite block, player 2 in the middle of free throw line and players 4 and 5 in a ballside stack in middle position.

Man-Man Baseline: Buck

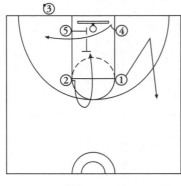

Diagram 1

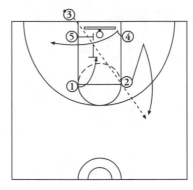

Diagram 2

Purpose:

To execute an effective baseline out of bounds play that is initiated from a box set.

Organization:

Player 1 v-cuts from opposite elbow to beyond the three-point area. Player 4 receives a cross-screen from player 5 and cuts to ballside corner. Player 2 loops from ballside elbow, receives a back screen from player 5 and cuts to the basket, looking for the pass from player 3 (diagram 1).

Variation:

Players 1 and 2 can interchange, which would result in the threat of a 3-point shooter. Player 3 makes the inbound pass to player 2 for the 3-point shot (diagram 2) instead of player 1 cutting to the basket.

Hot Tips

- Initial set up: player 3 is the inbound passer from under offensive basket.
- Players 5 and 2 set up on ballside (block and elbow respectively).
- Players 4 and 1 set up opposite ball (block and elbow respectively).

Man-Man Baseline: Platt Tech

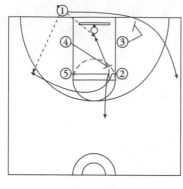

Diagram 1

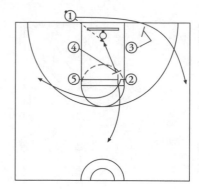

Diagram 2

Purpose:

To score on a baseline out of bounds play from a box set.

Organization:

Players 4 and 5 set a double screen for player 2, who comes off to ballside wing to receive the pass from player 1 and looks for a shot. Player 5 (who screened) steps out for ball reversal if necessary (diagram 1).

Variation:

Players 4 and 5 set a double screen for player 2, who cuts to ballside wing. Player 4 rolls to the basket after screen for player 2 for a pass and a lay-up from player 1. Player 5 steps out for ball reversal if necessary.

- Initial setup: player 1 takes the ball out of bounds.
- Players 4 and 5 set up on ballside (block and elbow respectively).
- Players 3 and 2 set up opposite ball (block and elbow respectively).

Man-Man Baseline: 35/53

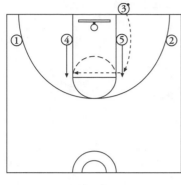

Diagram 1

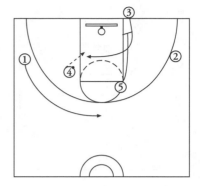

Diagram 2

Purpose:

To execute a baseline out of bounds play that will utilize a ball screen for the inbound passer or post player to score.

Organization:

Player 3 inbounds the ball on the baseline. Player 5 pops to ballside elbow looking to receive the pass from 3, while player 4 simultaneously pops to opposite elbow for ball reversal (diagram 1). Once player 4 receives the reversal pass from player 5, 5 downscreens for player 3 who curls to the middle from out of bounds looking for a pass from 4. Player 1 flashes to the top of the key from the left wing for defensive balance (diagram 2).

Variation:

Either call is "35" or "53"!

Hot Tips

- Lineup in a 1-4 flat across the baseline with player 5 being on ballside block
- Coach will call "35" or "53" to determine screener and cutter.
- A call of "35" indicates that player 3 uses 5 as a screen, and a call of "53" indicates that player 5 will use a screen set by 3.

Man-Man Baseline: Regular and Reverse

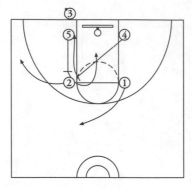

Diagram 1

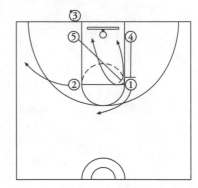

Diagram 2

Purpose:

To execute an effective box set man-man baseline out of bounds play that utilizes screen the screener concept.

Organization:

Player 2 cuts ballside corner off a backscreen from 5 (diagram 1).

- Option 1: Player 5 receives a cross screen from 4 and cuts down middle of lane.
- Option 2: Player 4 rolls to ballside basket, after screen for player 5.
- Option 3: Player 2 goes to corner and looks for pass from player 3.
- Option 4: Player 1 flashes the top of key for safety and defensive balance.

Variation:

Reverse: Player 4 backscreens for player 1, as 1 pops out to top of key (diagram 2).

- Option 1: Player 5 cross screens for 4, as 4 dives down the lane.
- Option 2: Player 5 rolls to ballside basket, after cross screen for 4.

- Initial setup is as follows: Player 3 inbounds the ball, player 5 is ballside block, player 2 is ballside elbow, player 4 is opposite block and player 1, opposite elbow.
- Opposite pass for post player will usually be open because the defense concentrates on the ballside player.

Mike Batell
Duke University

Man-Man Baseline: Drew Prep

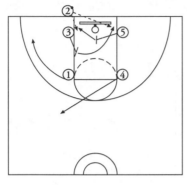

Diagram 1

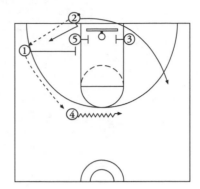

Diagram 2

Purpose:

To execute an effective baseline out of bounds play a box set that emphasizes screen the screener into a single-double screen.

Organization:

Player 3 upscreens for player 1, who pops to the ballside corner. Player 5 diagonal back screens for the screener (3), who cuts to opposite block. Player 4 clears out to ballside top of key. Player 2 looks for 3 or 5 (diagram 1).

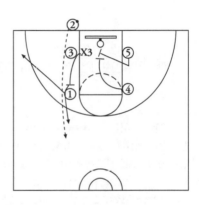

Diagram 3

Variations:

* If neither player 3 or 5 is open, then player 2
  passes to 1 and comes off either a single screen from 3 on left block, or, after 1 reverses to player 4 at the top, a double screen from 5 and 1 on the ballside (diagram 2).

* Down: After setting the screen for player 1, if player 3 reads the defender cheating underneath player 5's diagonal back screen, 3 calls "down." Player 5 changes the angle of the screen and combines with 4 to set a stagger double downscreen. Player 1 still flashes corner and 3 pops out to the 3-point area for shot (diagram 3).

Hot Tips

* Initial setup is as follows: Player 2 inbounds the ball, player 3 is on the ballside block, player 1 is on the ballside elbow, player 4 is on the opposite elbow and player 5, opposite block.

* As soon as the ball is slapped, players 3 and 5 leave spots to go screen. Player 1 needs to v-cut to get open. Player 3 sets a touch and go screen, slipping off player 5's back screen (diagram 1).

* Player 2 must read the defender for a set up and a possible, pop, curl or fade on either side (diagram 2).

Man-Man Baseline: Up

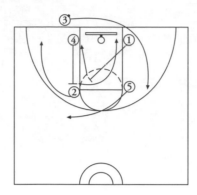

Diagram 1

Purpose:

To execute a baseline out of bounds play that is initiated from a box set and is a counter play for "Down."

Organization:

On the slap of the ball, player 4 moves first and sets an upscreen for the player 2, who cuts to ballside corner. A half-second later, player 1 sets a diagonal upscreen for player 4 (who comes off opposite to basket) and then rolls back to the ballside block. Player 5 serves as defensive balance, popping out high to three-point area. After the inbound pass is made, player 3 cuts baseline to opposite ballside mid-wing area (diagram 1).

Variations:

- The options are to pass to player 2 (ballside corner) jump shot, player 4 (opposite side) for lay-up the, player 1 on the pivot, rolling to ballside block, or player 5 for safety.
- Can be executed from both sides of the floor.

Hot Tips
- Timing is crucial.
- The inbounder must read the defense and utilize pass fakes.

Man-Man Baseline: Down

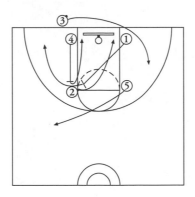

Diagram 1

Purpose:

To execute a baseline out of bounds play that is initiated from a box set and is a counter play for "Up."

Organization:

On the slap of the ball, player 1 moves first and sets a diagonal upscreen for the player 2, who cuts to opposite side of basket. A half-second later, player 4 sets an up screen for player 1 (who comes off to ballside corner) and then rolls back to the ballside block. Again, player 5 serves as defensive balance, popping out high to ballside three-point area. After the inbound pass is made, player 3 cuts baseline to opposite mid-wing area (diagram 1).

Variations:

- The options are to pass to player 2 (opposite) for the lay-up, player 1 (ballside corner) for jump shot, player 4 on the pivot, rolling to ballside block, or player 5 for safety.

- Can be executed from both sides of the floor.

Hot Tips
- Timing is crucial.
- The inbounder must read the defense and utilize pass fakes.

Man-Man Baseline: Double

Diagram 1

Diagram 2

Diagram 3

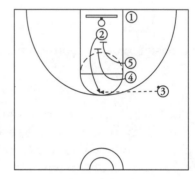

Diagram 4

Purpose:

To create a scoring opportunity for one of your primary shooters from an out of bounds play.

Organization:

Initial setup is with player 1 as the inbound passer (your second best shooter), players 5, 4 and 2 are in a stack on the strong side of the key, and player 3 on the weakside elbow. Player 2 is your best shooter (diagram 1). Player 2 curls around players 4 and 5, cutting into the center of the lane (diagram 2). Player 3 curls off a double screen from players 4 and 5, receiving the inbound pass from player 1 on the

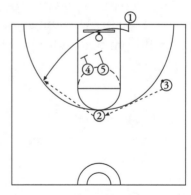

Diagram 5

ballside wing (diagram 3). Player 2 now cuts up the center of the lane (to beyond the three-point line) off another double screen from players 4 and 5. Player 3 passes to player 2 for a jump shot, as player 1 has now stepped inbounds (diagram 4).

Variation:

If the 2 does not have an open shot, 2 passes to the player 1 who has come off another double screen in the lane from the players 4 and 5 to the left wing for a jump shot (diagram 5).

- Player 2 may be open on the initial curl.
- Player 5 may be open after setting a screen for player 3.
- Players 4 and 5 need to set the screen for player 2, as the pass to the player 3 is in the air so 3 can catch and reverse the ball immediately.
- Players 4 and 5 now turn and immediately set the screens for player 1 who will have a short jump shot or curl.
- Players 4 and 5 might be open for a direct pass after setting any of the screens.

Bill McNally
Poly Prep

Man-Man Baseline: Combo

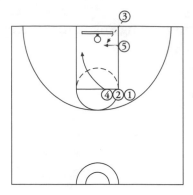

Diagram 1

Diagram 2

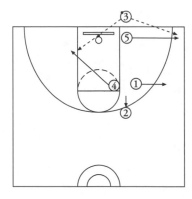

Diagram 3

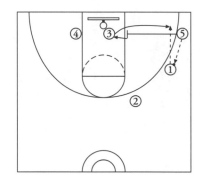

Diagram 4

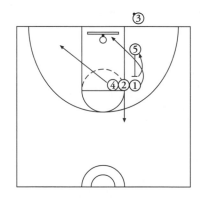

Diagram 5

Purpose:

To execute an baseline out of bounds play (with multiple options) that is highly effective against man-man and zone.

Organization:

- Options 1 and 2 vs. Man-to-Man — Player 5 is isolated for a one on one isolation or 5 can go across the lane to seal 5's defender (diagram 1).

- Option 3 vs. Man or Zone — Player 2 steps back, and players 4 and 1 pinch in to set a double screen for 2 who is looking for the 3-point shot (diagram 2).

- Option 4 vs. Man or Zone — Player 5 steps out to the corner for a pass, player 3 goes under the basket and player 1 then steps to the wing (diagram 3). Player 5 reverses the ball to player 1 and then screens in for player 3. Player 3 comes off player 5's screen for a corner 3-point shot (diagram 4).

Variations:

- vs. Man-to-Man — player 4 is able to cut opposite block for lay-up (diagram 1).

- Sometimes player 5 may be open, slipping the screen for a lay-up (diagram 4).
- Option 5 vs. Man-to-Man — a pressure release can be player 5 screening up the lane for player 1, who cuts ballside block. Player 5 then rolls to the basket (diagram 5).

 Hot Tip   Player 3 is the inbounds passer, player 5 sets up on ballside block, players 4, 2 and 1 set up in side by side at the ballside elbow (diagram 1).

Man-Man Baseline: #1

Diagram 1

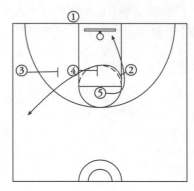

Diagram 2

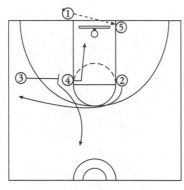

Diagram 3

Diagram 4

Diagram 5

Purpose:

To execute an effective inbound play that utilizes single or stagger double screens for the inbounder to shoot a jump shot.

Organization:

Initial setup begins with player 1 taking the ball out, player 2 on opposite block, player 3 in the ballside corner, player 4 at ballside block and player 5 at the free throw line (diagram 1). Player 2 screens for player 5, as 5 cuts to the opposite block (diagram 2). Players 4 and 3 set a stagger double screen for player 2, then player 4 rolls to the ballside block and player 3 pops out to top of key area for release (diagram 3). Player 1 passes to player 2, who immediately passes it up to player 3 (diagram 4).

Variation:

After pass is made to player 2 (and kicked up to player 3), player 1 either goes opposite off a screen from player 5 or comes off a stagger double ballside screen from players 4 and 2, (diagram 5).

Man-Man Baseline: 3-Series

Diagram 1

Diagram 2

Diagram 3

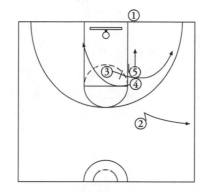

Diagram 4

Purpose:

To execute an effective man-man baseline out of bounds play that utilizes multiple options.

Organization:

Player 5 cuts opposite block and player 4 dives ballside block after a double screen for 3. Player 2 cuts high, right sideline (diagram 1).

Diagram 5

Variation:

- Player 3 backscreens for player 2, who cuts opposite block, continuing on to left corner (diagram 2).

- After screen for player 2, 3 comes of a double screen from players 5 and 4. Players 5 and 4 cut to respective spots (as shown in diagram 1) after a screen for player 3 (diagram 3).

- Player 3 screens for 4, then comes off a screen from player 5 (diagram 4).

- Player 3 screens for 5, who cuts opposite block, then dives to ballside block. Player 4 cuts toward right corner for quick shot (diagram 5).

Cory Furman, Assistant Coach
Goshen College

Man-Man Baseline: 3

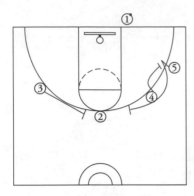

Diagram 1

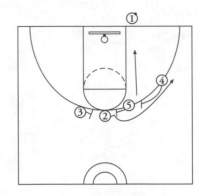

Diagram 2

Diagram 3

Diagram 4

Diagram 4

Purpose:

To execute an effective baseline out of bounds play that has numerous scoring options.

Organization:

Player 4 fakes a screen for 5, calling out player 5's name. This fluff screen initiates player 5 to go screen for player 2 at top. Prior to 5 moving, player 3 flashes to top, as to screen for 2. Player 2 fakes use of 3's screen (diagram 1). Player 2 comes off a stagger double screen from 5 and 4. Player 2 looks for a quick 3-point shot. If player 4's defender hedges out to stop 2, then 4 simply rolls to the basket (diagram 2). If both 2 and 4 are defended, player 5 clears out as outlet, while 3 l-cuts to opposite baseline (diagram 3).

Variation:

Counter – Player 4 actually screens for 5, who makes a sharp cut to the basket. At same time, player 3 screens for 2 and 2 comes off to left wing (diagram 4). If the team defends this counter, then 3 is outlet, while player 2 l-cuts opposite to get open. Player 4 l-cuts on ballside to get free and should have a post feed to player 5 (diagram 5).

Out of bounds Plays

Hot Tips

- Also used is screen the screener counter, where player 3 actually screens for 2, who goes opposite ball. Player 3 then continues on and comes off a stagger double screen from players 4 and 5 (who can then roll to basket).
- Simple play with numerous options.
- Use spacing properly and time your cuts. Make your cuts hard.

Jason Adkins
Colerain High School

Man-Man Baseline: Stack Low #2

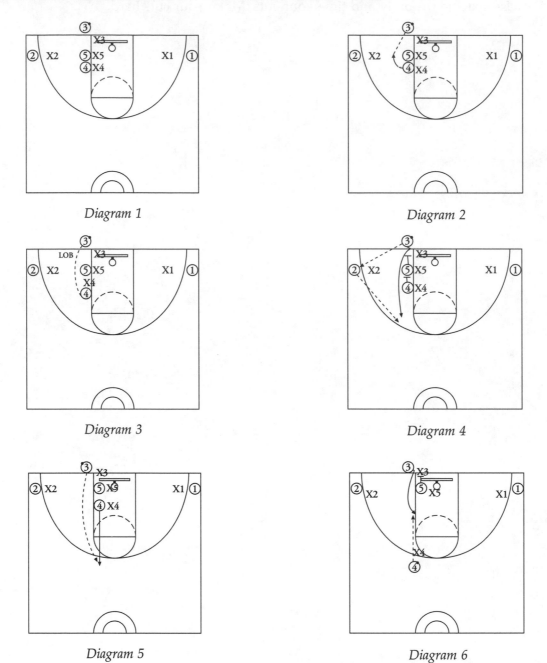

Diagram 1   Diagram 2

Diagram 3   Diagram 4

Diagram 5   Diagram 6

Purpose:

To execute a baseline out of bounds play that is effective against a man defense and utilizes a ballside stack to exploit a low post and perimeter scoring opportunity.

Organization:

This play starts with the same alignment as Stack Low #1. Player 5 ducks in to occupy X-5 (diagram 1). Player 3 reads how player 4 is being defended and then passes to 4 for a score (diagram 2).

Variation:

- Player 3 reads how player 4 is being defended and then lob passes to 4 for a score (diagram 3).
- If X-2 helps on players 4 or 5, player 3 passes to 2 in the ballside corner and receives a staggered double screen from 5 and 4, coming off up to the ballside top for a shot (diagram 4). Player 3 may also penetrate (make a scoring move) or pass to 4, who ducked in and sealed defender.

- Initial set is as follwing: player 3 is the inbound passer and good shooter, 5 is the low stack player on ballside stack and strongest post player, player 4 is the high stack player and athletic scorer, player 2 is the ballside corner and best shooter, and 1 is opposite corner and capable shooter.
- X-2 = (Ballside) 2-Guard Defender, X-1 = (Opposite) 1-Guard Defender, X-3 = 3-Inbound Passer Defender, X-5 = Center-Defender, and X-4 = (Ballside) Forward-Defender.
- Player 3 must pass to 4's target hand, avoiding the defender (diagram 2).
- If X-2 or X-1, help defend the post players (4 or 5) then wherever player 3 passes the ball (to 2 or 1), players 4 and 5 set a stagger double screen for 3 (diagram 4).
- Player 4 releases to the elbow if 2 is unavailable. Player 5 screens X-3, and player 3 reads the defense. Player 4 passes to player 3 to score.

Baseline Zone: Curl

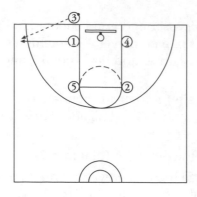

Diagram 1

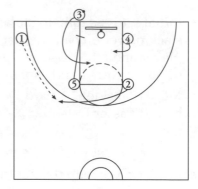

Diagram 2

Purpose:

To execute a baseline out of bounds play for a quick inside score against a zone defense, with a screen.

Organization:

As the play begins in a box alignment, player 3 inbounds the ball, and player 1 pops out to ballside corner for the pass (diagram 1). As player 1 receives the pass, player 2 pops to the left top of the key for the pass. As player 2 receives the pass, player 5 downscreens for the player 3 curling in from out of bounds looking for the dump down. Player 4 cuts in to rebound (diagram 2).

Hot Tips

- The box alignment begins the play as player 1 starts on the ballside block, player 4 is opposite block, player 5 is ballside elbow, and player 2 is opposite elbow.
- Player 3 can come from out of bounds and score quickly.
- Player 4 can crash the boards from weak side.

Jason Adkins
Colerain High School

Baseline Zone: Stack Low #1

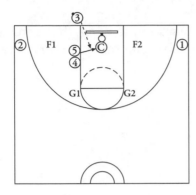

Diagram 1

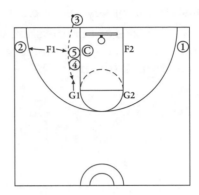

Diagram 2

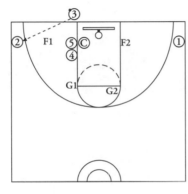

Diagram 3

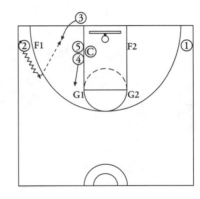

Diagram 4

Purpose:

To execute a baseline out of bounds play that is effective against a zone defense and utilizes a ballside stack to exploit a low post or a perimeter scoring opportunity.

Organization:

Player 3 pass fakes to 1 in the opposite corner. Simultaneously, player 5 ducks in front of C and then receives the pass from 3 to score (diagram 1).

Variation:

- If pass to player 5 is unavailable, then player 3 looks to lob pass to 4, who splits the gap between the F-1, C and G-1 defenders (diagram 2).

- If pass to player 4 is unavailable, then player 3 passes to 2 in ballside corner for a shot (diagram 3).

- If player 2 has no shot, then 2 dribbles hard to the wing, as player 3 steps into ballside short-corner looking for return pass, and a shot or post feed to player 5, who has ducked in front of C. Player 4 steps up to mid-post (diagram 4).

- Initial set is as follows: player 3 is the inbound passer and good shooter, player 5 low stack player on ballside stack and strongest post player, player 4 high stack player and athletic scorer, player 2 is ballside corner and best shooter, and player 1 is opposite corner and capable shooter.

- G-1 = (Ballside) Top Guard Defender, G-2 = (Opposite) Guard Defender, F-1 = (Ballside) Bottom Forward Defender, C = Center Defender, and F-2 = (Opposite) Forward Defender.

- Player 3 must pass fake to 1, so F-2 is kept alert (diagram 1).

- If player 2 does shoot then player 5 takes rebounding responsibility on low (ballside) block boxing out C. Player 4 takes rebounding responsibility for opposite block, boxing out F-2. Player 1 must flash to top of key for defensive balance (diagram 3).

- As soon as F-1 closes out on the shot, player 2 must dribble hard to the wing, thus forcing F-1 to release and G-1 to pick up. At the point of exchange, player 3 has stepped in and received the reversal pass from 2 (diagram 4).

Baseline Zone: "I"

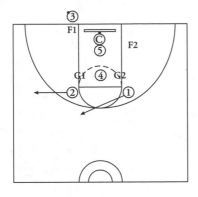

Diagram 1

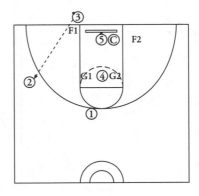

Diagram 2

Diagram 3

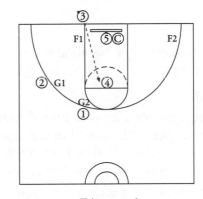

Diagram 4

Purpose:

   To execute a baseline out of bounds play that is effective against a 2-3 zone defense and utilizes a "3-across" free throw alignment to exploit a low post and perimeter scoring opportunity.

Organization:

   Player 5 ducks in front of C for pass from player 3 and looks to score. Player 2 sprints to ballside wing area, as 1 sprints to top of key area (diagram 1). Player 3 reads G-1. If G-1 does not go with player 2, then player 3 passes to 2 for a quick shot or post feed to 5 (diagram 2).

Variation:

- If G-1 goes with player 2, and G-2 is below player 4, then 4 screens G-2 and player 3 passes to 1 for a shot (diagram 3).

- If G-1 and G-2 match-up on players 2 and 1, respectively, then player 4 flashes to middle of lane, receiving a pass from 3 for a score (diagram 4).

- G-1 = (Ballside) Top Guard Defender, G-2 = (Opposite) Guard Defender, F-1 = (Ballside) Bottom Forward Defender, C = Center Defender, and F-2 = (Opposite) Forward Defender.

- When player 5 steps in front of C, 5 reverse pivots to seal defender (diagram 1).

Baseline Zone: Two Back

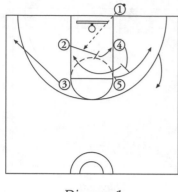

Diagram 1

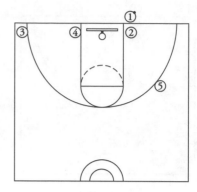

Diagram 2

Purpose:

To execute an effective baseline out of bounds play verses a man-man defense, utilizing screen the screener concept.

Organization:

Player 4 screens for player 5, who cuts to ballside corner and then up right sideline for release. Player 2 comes across to screen player 4 in the middle of the lane and then slips to the ball. Player 3 cuts to opposite corner. Player 1 blocks and then slips back to rim on opposite side (diagram 1).

- Option 1 – Player 1 passes to 4 on opposite block.
- Option 2 – Player 1 passes to 2 slipping to ballside block.
- Option 3 – Player 1 passes to 3 cutting to opposite corner.
- Option 4 – Player 1 passes to 5 for release (diagram 2).

 Initial set up is as follows: player 1 is the inbound passer, player 3 is on the opposite elbow, player 5 is on the ballside elbow, player 2 is the opposite block, and player 4 is on the ballside block.

Baseline Zone: "3"

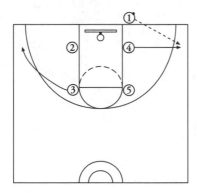

Diagram 1

Diagram 2

Diagram 3

Purpose:

To execute an effective baseline out of bounds play verses a man-man defense, initializing from a box set.

Organization:

Player 1 passes to player 4, who has cut to ballside corner. Player 3 cuts to opposite elbow (diagram 1). Player 5 downscreens for player 2. Player 4 reverses the ball to 2 at top of key (diagram 2). After the screen, player 5 seals defender in paint. Player 4 downscreens for player 1, the inbounder (diagram 3).

- Option 1 – Player 2 looks for 5 in the lane.
- Option 2 – Player 2 looks for 1 coming off of 4's screen.

Hot Tip Initial set up is as follows: Player 1 is the inbound passer, player 3 is on the opposite elbow, player 5 is on the ballside elbow, player 2 is the opposite block, and player 4 is the ballside block.

Baseline Zone: 1-Cutter

Diagram 1

Diagram 2

Purpose:

To execute an effective baseline out of bounds play that focuses on player 1 cutting to the basket verses a 2-3 zone.

Organization:

Player 2 inbounds the ball, as player 5 lines up on ballside block. Player 4 is ballside, short corner; 3 is ballside, three-point line, and player 1 is behind 3 (diagram 1). Player 4 pops out ballside corner, player 5 flashes opposite block. Player 3 cuts to ballside wing, and player 1 cuts down middle of lane for pass from 2 (diagram 2).

Variation:

If player 4's defender collapses on player 1 cutting, then 4 will be open for a shot in the corner (diagram 2).

Player 1 sets up the defender by cutting opposite and then flashing to the middle.

Baseline Zone: Pasci

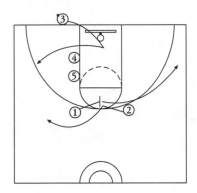

Purpose:

To execute an effective baseline out of bounds play that is set up for the inbound passe to score.

Organization:

On player 3's signal, player 5 breaks in the lane under the basket. Player 1 sets a cross screen for player 2, who cuts to ballside top, as 1 continues to opposite corner. Once the ball is inbounded, player 3 v-cuts in the lane, takes his defender off of player 4's screen and pops to ballside corner.

Variation:

If a 3 point-shot is needed then 3 pops out to the 3-point area in the corner.

- Initial setup is as follows: Player 3 inbounds the ball. Player 4 and 5 are in a ballside stack. Player 1 is on the ballside top of key, and player 2, the opposite top of key.
- Player 3 can look to player 5 on the cut in or looks to 5 on the cut in or out top to player 2.

Sideline: Paul VI

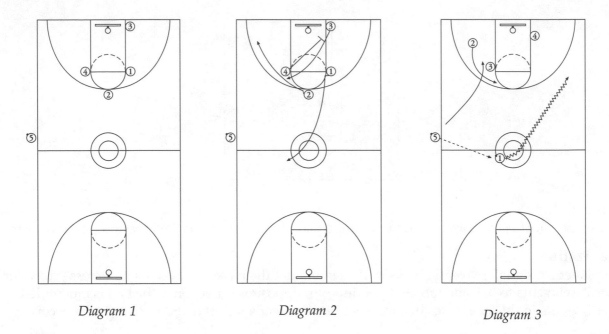

Diagram 1   Diagram 2   Diagram 3

Purpose:

To execute an effective sideline out of bounds play that utilizes multiple options.

Organization:

Player 5 inbounds the ball. Player 2 (the scoring guard) is at top of key. Player 4 is on the ballside elbow, and player 1 is weakside elbow. Player 3 is weakside block (diagram 1). Player 2 moves first, going hard off 4 to ballside, midcorner for pass. Player 1 comes back as far as needed. Player 4 downscreens for 3, who flashes to top. Player 5 can pass to the first open player and look for options (diagram 2).

Variation:

If player 5 passes to 1, go into quick score option, where players 5 and 3 screen for 2, as player 1 takes the ball hard to 4's side. Player 1 looks for 4 or 2 (diagram 3).

The pass to player 1 presents two scoring options: a pass to post or to a shooter coming opposite off a screen.

Sideline: Kentucky

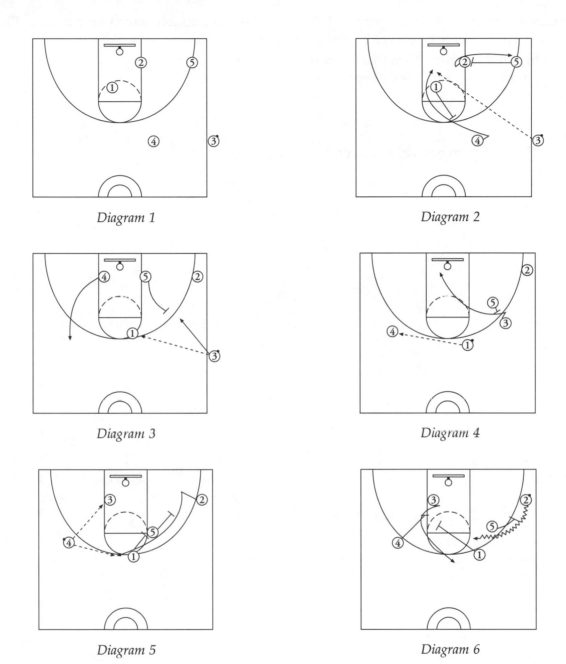

Diagram 1

Diagram 2

Diagram 3

Diagram 4

Diagram 5

Diagram 6

Purpose:
To score on a lob pass from a sideout set up.

Organization:
Players align as follows: Player 3 inbounds the ball to player 1 in the middle of the lane. Player 2 sets up a ballside block. Player 5 is in the ballside corner, and player 4 lines up straight across from player 3 (see diagram 1). Player 1 then backscreens for player 4. Player 5 screens for player 2 and then looks to pass to player 4 from over the top (see diagram 2).

Variations:

- If player 4 does not receive the lob pass, player 1 steps to the ball and receives the pass from 3. Player 4 comes out to the opposite wing and player 5 backscreens for player 3 (see diagram 3).

- If player 3 shuffle cuts off player 5's backscreen, then player 1 reverses to player 4 on the wing (see diagram 4).

- After player 4 receives the pass, players 1 and 5 set a stagger double screen for player 2. Player 4 looks for player 3 inside or player 2 coming off the screens (see diagram 5).

- On pass to 2 in the corner, 3 shuffles off player 4. Player 5 sets a ball screen on 2, as 4 and 1 set a stagger double screen for 3 (see diagram 6).

Player 4 goes backdoor if overplayed (see diagram 4).

Sideline: Oscoda

Diagram 1

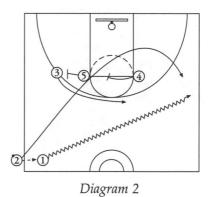

Diagram 2

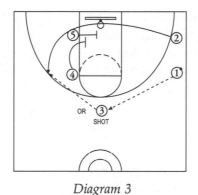

Diagram 3

Purpose:

To execute an effective sideline out of bounds play that will result in numerous scoring opportunities.

Organization:

Initial set up is as follows: player 2 (the best shooter) is the inbound passer. Players 4 and 5 are post players at the opposite and ballside elbow. Player 1 is lined up in front of 2. Player 3 lined up ballside corner (diagram 1). Player 2 passes to player 1, and cuts to opposite (right) corner, as player 1 dribbles hard to opposite (right) wing. Players 4 and 5 set a set double stagger screen for player 3 (diagram 2). Player 1 makes a reverse pass to player 3 (coming off the screens) for a jump shot at top of key (diagram 3).

Variation:

If player 3 is not open for a shot, then 3 makes an additional pass to player 2 (on left wing) coming off another set of double stagger screens from players 4 and 5 for a jump shot (diagram 3).

Screens and cuts must be timed.

Sideline: Deep Corner

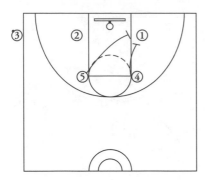

Diagram 1

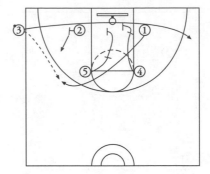

Diagram 2

Purpose:

To execute an effective sideline out of bounds play that is executed from an awkward position on the floor. This play is initiated out of box set and utilizes a serious of triple screens and staggered double screens to free the inbound passer for an open shot.

Organization:

Players 4 and 5 break down to set a staggered double screen for 1, who comes to the left wing to receive the pass from 3. After the inbounds pass to player 1, 3 cuts off three back screens from 2, 5 and 4 to the right corner (diagram 1). Player 1 dribbles the ball to the top and hits 3 in the right corner for a

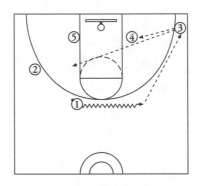

Diagram 2

shot. Player 4 looks to post, as 5 flares to the left block and 2 pops out to the right wing (diagram 2).

Variation:

Player 1 passes to 3 for the shot, or
- 3 can pass to 4 for low post score
- 3 can skip pass to 2 for a perimeter shot or a quick pass into 5, posting.

- After the pass is made to player 1, 2 must step out to set the first back screen for 3. After setting the staggered double screen for 1, 5 and 4 immediately turn in the lane and set the second and third back screens for 3 (diagram 1).
- After the third back screen, 4 turns and seals defender on ballside block. Following the second back screen for 2, 5 flashes to opposite block for a possible pass from 2. Upon first back screen for 3, 2 has popped out to the left wing and sets up for a skip pass from 3 (diagram 2).

Sideline: Arizona

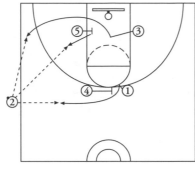

Diagram 1

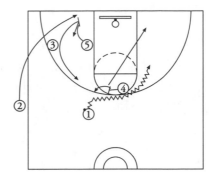

Diagram 2

Diagram 3

Purpose:
To execute a side out of bounds play with multiple options.

Organization:
Player 2 inbounds the ball. Player 5 sets up on ballside block and sets screen for player 3, then rolls back. Player 3 flashes from weak-side block and cuts to ballside corner. Player 4 sets up on the ballside elbow and screens across for player 1. Player 1 flashes to ballside top of the key. The options continue from here (diagram 1). Player 2 passes to player 1, and then comes off a stagger double screen by players 3 and 5. Player 1 can rub off a screen from player 4 and turn the corner. Player 3 sets first screen and then clears to right side for balance (diagram 2). Player 3 clears after screen and player 4 sets a screen for player 3. Player 2 shoots or looks for player 5 (diagram 3).

Variations:
- Player 4 can roll to the basket, step back for kick or a pop, and open side for player 1. Player 1 can cross back to left and look for player 2 off a stagger (diagram 2).
- Player 1 can pass to player 3 and then flare off a screen set by player 2 (diagram 3).

- Enter to player 5, 3 or 1!
- If ball goes to player 5, look for a shot.
- If ball goes to player 3, look to player 5.
- If ball goes to player 1 in high post, run series.

Hot Tips

Sideline: "A"

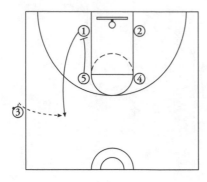

Diagram 1

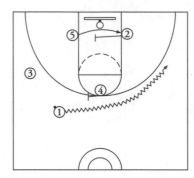

Diagram 2

Diagram 3

Diagram 4

Purpose:

To execute an effective man-man sideline out of bounds play that initiates from a "box set" alignment and utilizes screen the screener action exploiting both a perimeter and post scoring option.

Organization:

Player 5 down screens for 1, who pops out to top to receive pass from 3 (diagram 1). Player 4 ballscreens for 1, as 2 cross screens for 5 in the low post (diagram 2). After the ballscreen for player 1, player 4 downscreens for 2 (diagram 3).Player 1 can look to hit 2 for open shot or pass to 5 in the low post for isolation (diagram 4).

Variation:

If player 1 is denied the pass, 5 pops out to receive pass and runs hand-off action with 3 (diagram 1).

Initial setup is as follows: player 3 is the inbound passer, 1 is ballside block, 2 is opposite block, 5 is ballside elbow, and 4 is opposite elbow.

Sideline: Seminoles

Diagram 1

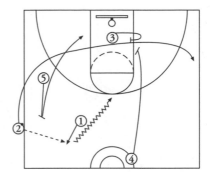

Diagram 2

Purpose:

To execute a sideline out of bounds play verses a man-man defense that exploits the lob pass for a quick score.

Organization:

Player 2 is the inbound pass as player 5 flashes from ballside block to wing. Player 4 flashes out to half-court area from opposite block, as player 1 backscreens for player 3, who looks to receive the lob pass for lay-up (diagram 1).

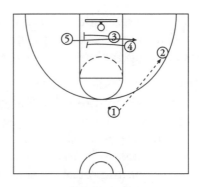

Diagram 3

Variation:

No Lob – Player 1 slips in to receive the inbound pass from player 2 and attacks the middle with a dribble. Player 5 backscreens for player 2 and then rolls back to the basket (left side). Players 3 and 4 set a double screen for player 2, coming out to the right wing for a jump shot (diagram 2). Player 1 passes to player 2, as players 3 and 4 set a double cross screen on opposite block for player 5. Player 5 flashes hard to ballside post. Player 2 looks to pass to player 5 for a score (diagram 3).

Hot Tips

- The initial set is player 2 in bounding the ball; player 1 is at the free throw line, player 3 straight across from 2, player 5 on the ballside post and player 4 opposite block.
- Post players walk defenders up and break to safety (diagram 1).
- Player 2 must slip through player 3 and 4's screen for a jump shot in the corner (diagram 2).
- Players 3 and 4 cross screen and slip into motion (diagram 3).

Sideline: Bryan

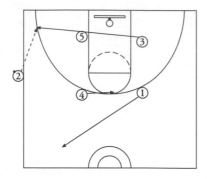

Diagram 1

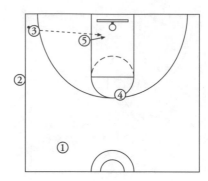

Diagram 2

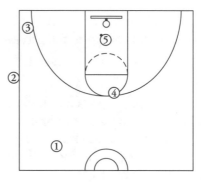

Diagram 3

Purpose:

To execute an effective sideline out of bounds play that is initiated from a box set and utilizes a baseline, ballside cut to free up the post player for a score.

Organization:

Player 3 runs baseline from the right block to the left corner off of 5's block screen. Player 4 cross screens for 1 at the opposite elbow (diagram 1). Player 2 passes the ball to 3. Player 1 becomes a safety outlet after coming off of 4's screen (diagram 2). Player 3 passes to 5 in low post, who sealed defender after screen (diagram 3).

Hot Tips

- Initial setup is as follows: player 2 inbounds the ball, 5 is ballside block, 4 is ballside elbow, 3 is opposite block and 1 is opposite elbow.
- Player 5 turns and screens for 3 cutting baseline (diagram 1).
- Player 5 must pivot and seal the defender after 3 cuts off 5's screen (diagram 2).

Sideline: Canyon

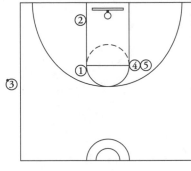

Diagram 1

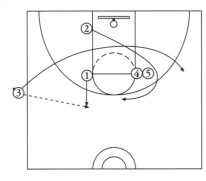

Diagram 2

Diagram 3

Purpose:

   To execute an effective sideline out of bounds play that utilizes basket cuts and continues into a three-out, two-in motion.

Organization:

   Player 1 sets up at ballside elbow. Player 2 sets up on the ballside block for the post up option. Player 3 is the inbound passer. Players 4 and 5 stack up on the opposite elbow (diagram 1). Player 1 steps away holding the defending. Player 2 looks to post up and then curls off a stack screen from players 4 and 5 for a shot at the stop of the key. Player 3 passes to 1 and cuts hard for a lay-up/ return pass and then continues to the opposite corner or wing (diagram 2). After the initial screen for player 2, player 4 cuts to the left block as player 5 drops to the opposite block. Player 1 dribbles to the wing and — if no pass is made to player 3 or 2 — looks for 4 in the post. Player 2 stays at the top of the key. Player 3 sets up on the opposite wing after continuing through.

Sideline: Side Out

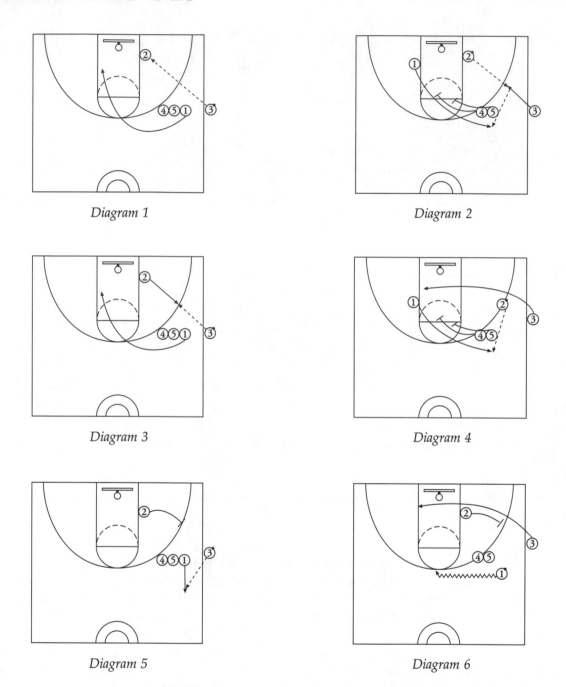

Diagram 1

Diagram 2

Diagram 3

Diagram 4

Diagram 5

Diagram 6

Purpose:

To create a scoring opportunity from a sideline out of bounds possession.

Organization:

Player 3 inbounds the ball, player 2 is at the ballside block, players 1-4-5 are lined up straight in this order toward 3. As the ball is handed to player 3, player 1 rolls off 5 and 4 to the weakside post. Player 3 passes to 2 (diagram 1). Player 3 steps inbounds for the return pass from player 2. Player 2 may be open for the jump shot. After player 1 clears, players 4 and 5 turn and set a stagger

176

Diagram 7

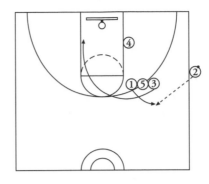

Diagram 8

Diagram 9

double screen for 1 coming back to the top and possibly getting a 3-point look (diagram 2). If player 2 is doubled in the post, then player 3 breaking to the ball will create an open pass. Player 3 cuts baseline for a hand-off and if not received must continue weakside for rebounding position (diagram 3). Players 1, 4 and 5 continue the same action as in diagram 2, but player 1 will look for the pass from 2 instead of 3 (diagram 4).

Variations:

- Point Guard Option – If the second pass cannot be made, player 1 pops out toward half-court. Player 2 breaks toward the ball and becomes a screener (diagram 5).
- Player 1 receives the pass from player 3, who receives a backscreen from player 2 and continues on to the left wing for a shot. Player 1 dribbles hard left looking for 3 (diagram 6).
- Players 5 and 4 set a stagger double screen for 2. Player 1 looks for player 2 for the 3-point shot or 5 (the first screener) slipping to the basket (diagram 7).
- Player 2 inbounds the ball. Player 4 starts on the ballside block. Players 1, 5 and 3 are lined up straight in this order toward 2. Player 3 rolls off 1 and 5 to weak-side rebounding position. Player 1 pops out toward half-court to receive a pass from player 2 (diagram 8).
- As player 1 receives the pass from 2, player 4 steps out from right block to set a flare (back) screen for 2. Player 5 sets a ballscreen for 1, giving the option of passing to player 2 for a shot or drive to the basket (diagram 9).

Hot Tips

- Called "side out" because all options create a scoring opportunity and the entire team needs to run.
- Although there are different reads, it is effective verses both the man and zone defenses.
- Must have inbounds passer who is able to hit the three-point shot.
- Creates a couple of options for end of game situations.
- Post up the team's best guard to create a mismatch.
- Stack other players in front of the passer.

Section Four:
Full-court Offense

Press Break: Tigers

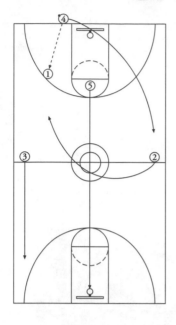

Diagram 1

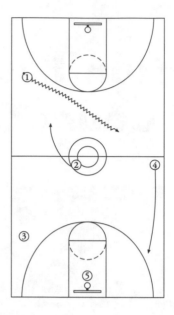

Diagram 2

Purpose:

To execute an effective press break offense that leads to an initial scoring opportunity or early offense.

Organization:

Initial set-up has player 4 make the inbound pass to player 1 and then cut up the left sideline. Player 5 starts at the front court free throw line and sprints up the floor to underneath the basket. Player 3 starts at the right front side of half-court and sprints to the right sideline. Player 2 starts at the left front side of half-court and curls into the middle of half-court. Player 1 is on the free throw line extended on the ballside (diagram 1). Player 1 receives the pass from player 4 and attacks to the left. Player 2 curls back around 1 for a pass. Player 4 sprints up to the left sideline (diagram 2).

Hot Tip   As player 1 is attacking to the left side with a dribble, player 2 should use the loop curl to get behind 1 for a better passing angle on the reverse.

Barry Brodzinski
Paul VI High School

Press Break: Full-court Vs. Man or Zone Press

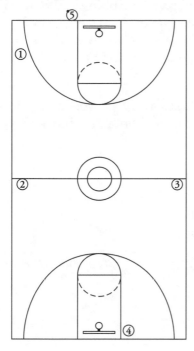

Diagram 1

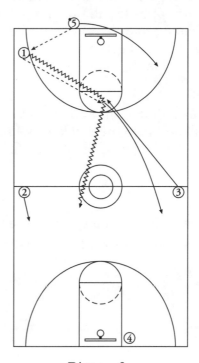

Diagram 2

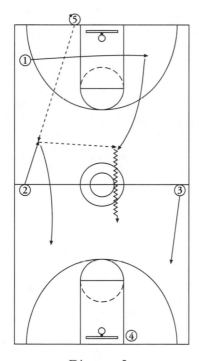

Diagram 3

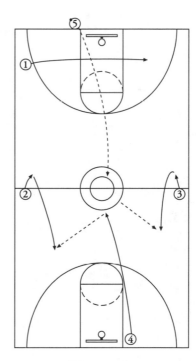

Diagram 4

Purpose:

To execute an effective full-court press break verses any press.

Organization:

Initial setup is with player 5 inbounding the ball, player 1 (best ballhandler) at ballside midpost extended area, players 2 and 3 lined at half-court (ballside and opposite, respectively) and player 4 in front court opposite ball (diagram 1). Player 5 passes to 1. Player 1 dribbles to the middle or hits player 3 flashing middle from opposite, who begins fast break. Player 5 goes opposite ball (diagram 2). If player 1 cannot get the ball, 1 clears out opposite and player 2 breaks toward the ball. Player 5 inbounds to 2. Player 2 passe to 1, who has curled back middle to start fast break (diagram 3).

Variation:

- Last second shot – Same alignment as above, but player 1 fakes away, players 2 and 3 step toward ball and then break deep, as 4 flashes up to half-court from front court block. Player 5 passes to 4, who passes it to 2 or 3 for a shot (diagram 4).

- When flashing make sure the cuts are hard and quick.
- Passes to a cutting player are key to start the break.

Press Break: "K"

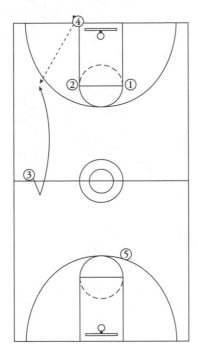

Diagram 1

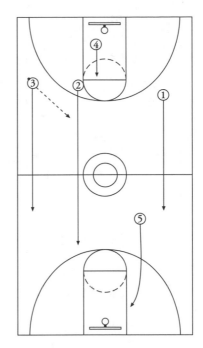

Diagram 2

Purpose:

To execute an effective full-court press break against a man/zone defense.

Organization:

Player 3 fakes going long and sprints to ballside 3-point area to receive pass from player 4 (diagram 1). Player 3 passes to player 2, who has sprinted up to half-court and begins fast break with 3 filling the right lane, player 4 trailing to the high post, player 5 diving to right block and player 1 the left wing (diagram 2).

Variations:

Player 2 either has fast break lay-up; hits player 3 on the right wing, passes to player 5 diving to the basket, makes a reversal passes to player 4 in the high post, or skip passes to player 1 to reset the offense (diagram 3).

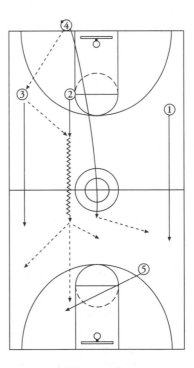

Diagram 3

- Initial set is with player 4 inbounding the ball. Player 2 (fastest player) ballside free throw line, player 3 (scorer) is on the ballside half-court, player 5 is in the front court at the 3-point line, and player 1 is on the opposite elbow.

- Player 3 must not get trapped and when pass is received, player 2 must push the ball up the floor hard and fast.

Press Break: Husky

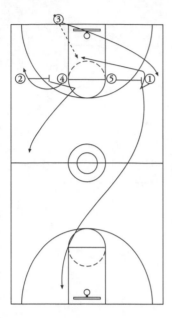

Diagram 1

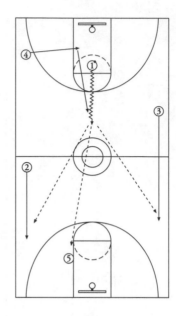

Diagram 2

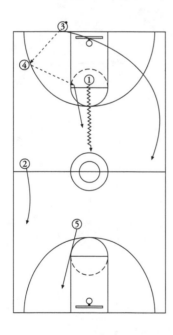

Diagram 3

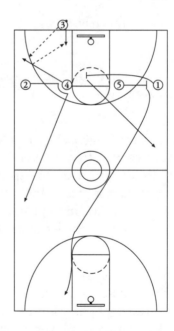

Diagram 4

Purpose:

To execute an effective full-court, press break that transitions into fast break offense. This 1-4 aligned press offense utilizes screens and is effective verses a man or zone defense.

Organization:

Option 1: Point Guard – Player 2 screens in for player 4 on the ballside elbow. Player 4 pops out to the right wing where player 2 started, and 2 must cut middle, running through and up the right sideline. Player 5 screens out to left wing for player 1 then sprints the left sideline, diving to the right block after getting to front court (top of key). Player 1 cuts hard in the middle of the lane off player 5's screen, looking to receive the pass from player 3 (diagram 1). If player 3 passes to player 1 and then fills the left wing, player 1 pushes the ball up the middle of floor looking ahead to player 2, 3 or 5. Player 4 is the trailer on the fast break (diagram 2).

Option 2: 3-man – Player 3 passes to 4 and then steps back in from out of bounds to initiate the break, with all players running their lanes. Player 1 must cut off player 5's screen and just fill player 3's original (left) lane. Player 3 pushes the ball hard up the middle of the floor, looking ahead to player 2, 5 or 1. Player 4 is the trailer on the fast break (diagrams 3 and 4).

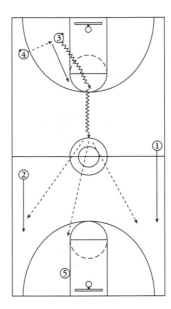

Diagram 5

Variation:

If player 1 does not receive the pass from player 3, then 3 passes to player 4 in the midcorner area and continue to fills opposite (left) lane. Player 4 receives the pass and immediately passes to player 1 in the middle to initiate the fast break (diagram 5).

- Initial setup has player 3 inbounding the ball on the baseline, while player 2 lines up ballside free throw line extended out side the 3-point line. Player 1 is set up in the same manner as player 2, but opposite the ball. Player 4 is on the ballside elbow and player 5 is on the weakside elbow.
- Player 4 must not flash down to the deep corner in a trap area.
- All players must run their lanes and not stay in another player's lane.
- Players 1 and 3 must be your best ballhandlers.

Gary DeCesare
University of Richmond

Fast Break: Ravens

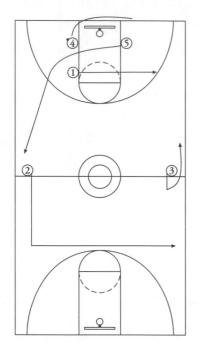

Diagram 1

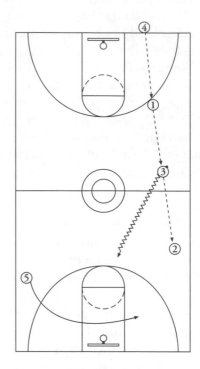

Diagram 2

Purpose:

To execute an effective sideline fast break transition offense after a (made or missed) foul shot.

Organization:

Player 4 inbounds the ball on left side as player 1 releases across court to left sideline for an outlet from player 4. After made free throw, player 5 releases from the block, running deep along the right sideline. Player 2 makes an l-cut, and player 3 comes back for the pass from player 1 (diagram 1). Player 4 passes to player 1, who hits player 3 at half-court. Player 3 hits player 2 or can dribble in for a 3-player fast break (5-3-2). Player 2 can pass to player 5 posting (diagram 2).

Variation:

- Missed free throw: Whichever side gets the rebound, that is the sideline. Player 1 goes to for the outlet. Whichever sideline player 1 goes to, that is who comes back to half-court to player 2 or player 3 for outlet.

- Whatever side player 1 is lined up on, that side takes the ball out on a made foul shot.
- Player 1 is the point guard, players 4 and 5 are the big men and players 2 and 3 guards.
- Players 4 and 5 must box out.
- Player 1 boxes out the shooter.
- Players 2 and 3 both release long when foul shot is released.
- Play can be executed with 4 players on the line and one player back at the middle of half-court.

Fast Break: Florida State

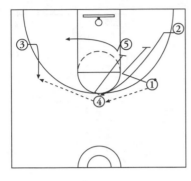

Diagram 1

Diagram 2

Purpose:

To execute an early offense off the fast break.

Organization:

From the right wing, player 1 reverses the ball to player 4, who immediately passes to player 3 on the left wing. Player 5 flashes to ballside (left) block. Player 1 and player 4 set a stagger double screen for player 2 coming to the top of key (diagram 1). Player 1 clears through to left short corner after screen for player 2. Player 3 passes to player 2 at the top, then cuts off a backscreen from player 5. After setting the stagger screen, player 4 pops out to the

Diagram 3

right wing (diagram 2). After the reversal from player 2 to player 4, 2 immediately downscreens for player 1. Player 5, after flashing high, turns and sets an additional screen for player 1. Player 1 pops to the top of key for shot (diagram 3).

Hot Tips

- This is at the end of the fast break and the initial setup is as follows: Player 1 with ball on right wing, player 2 in right corner, player 5 initial ballside block player 3 left wing, and player 4 trailer (top of key).
- Player 5 must set a backscreen and follow the ball to the free throw line (diagram 2).

Fast Break: Regular Series

Diagram 1

Diagram 2

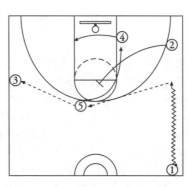

Diagram 3

Purpose:

To execute an effective fast break transition offense that leads into secondary offense.

Organization:

Player 5 inbounds the ball and is trailer (on the left side). Player 2 sprints the floor and gets to the right corner. Player 4 sprints and gets to right block. Player 1 dribbles the ball up the right side of the floor and looks for the 3-point shot. Player 3 sprints the left sideline and looks to score (diagram 1).

Variations:

- High Pick and Roll – Out of regular set, player 5 comes across to execute a pick and roll with player 1, who has read the defense while dribbling down the right sideline. Player 2 stays at the three-point line extended, while 3 spots up on the other wing (diagram 2).

- Ball Reversal – If player 2 doesn't receive the pass, player 1 passes to 5 at top, who reverses the ball to player 3 on the left wing. As the ball is reversed to 3, player 4 comes over to left block. Player 2 back screens for 5, (who cuts to opposite block) and then pops out to the top (diagram 3).

Hot Tips

- Everybody runs the floor hard! Player 5 is the inbound passer at all times.
- Player 5 rolls to the basket out of the pick and roll with 1. Player 1 looks to penetrate and kick if the pick and roll is covered (diagram 2).
- Player 3 looks for the 4 in the low post or for the lob pass to player 5 (diagram 3).

Fast Break: 3 Series

Diagram 1

Diagram 2

Purpose:

To execute an effective secondary fast break offense that leads to a low post or perimeter scoring opportunity.

Organization:

Player 3 dribbles the ball up in transition, as player 4 cuts from right block to left block. Player 2 backscreens for 5, (who cuts to right block) and then pops out to the top. Player 3 looks for 4 or 5 for the lob pass (diagram 1).

Variation:

Option: Pick and Roll with 3 – Out of regular set, player 5 comes across to execute a pick and roll with 3, as player 1 screens away for 2. Player 3 looks for the 5 on the pick and roll or player 2 coming to the top (diagram 2).

Hot Tips

- Everybody runs the floor hard! Player 5 is the inbound passer at all times.
- Same as "Regular Series," only use if the ball cannot be inbounded to player 1 (diagram 1).

Fast Break: Through Series

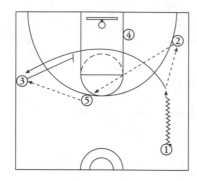

Diagram 1

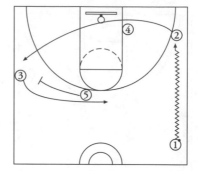

Diagram 2

Purpose:

To execute an effective secondary fast break offense that leads to a perimeter scoring opportunity.

Organization:

Player 1 passes to 2 in the corner, cuts through the lane, receives a downscreen from player 3 and fades to the left wing. Player 4 posts hard on ballside block. Player 2 skip passes to 5, who immediately passes to player 1 for a shot (diagram 1).

Diagram 3

Variations:

- Option: Dribble Series – Player 1 dribbles to player 2, forcing 2 to cut baseline to the opposite wing.
  On the dribble, player 5 sets a cross screen for player 3, who pops out to the top. Player 1 looks for 4 posting or 3 at the top (diagram 2).

- Option: 2 Runs Baseline – If player 1 does not dribble baseline, player 2 is waved to cut baseline, receiving a backscreen from 4 on the ballside block and 3 (who down screens). Player 5 sets a ballscreen for 1 and rolls to the basket as player 1 dribbles off looking for 2 in the left corner for a shot (diagram 3).

- Everybody runs the floor hard! Player 5 is the inbound passer at all times.
- Player 1 must make the decision to dribble to the corner (diagram 2).

Fast Break: Break 1

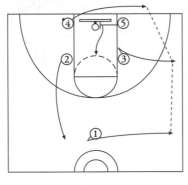

Diagram 1

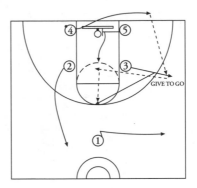

Diagram 2

Purpose:

To execute an effective fast break out of a free throw shooting alignment that avoids full-court defensive pressure.

Organization:

Player 1 roams above half-court, as player 4 inbounds the ball running the baseline. Player 5 will step under the basket, screen any defender, who is trying match-up with 4, and then run up the middle of the floor. Player 3 releases from free throw line, popping out to ballside sideline (left) to receive the pass from 4. Player 3 immediately passes to 1 so the fast break transition can begin. On the shot, player 2 releases from free throw line, cutting up right sideline, looks for a lay-up pass from 1 (diagram 1).

Variation:

If player 3 can not get pass to player 1, 3 and 5 will execute a give and go where 3 will quickly pass to 5 (running the middle of the floor) and cut to middle to receive a pass back from 5, thus initiating the break. Option: Player 3 can pass to 1 on the left side or player 2 streaking down the left side (diagram 2).

Hot Tips

- Initial set-up is as follows: Player 4 (low block) and player 2 (high post) are on the left side of the free throw line, player 5 (low block) and player 3 (high post) are on the right side of the free throw line. Player 1 roams above half-court.
- First priority is to box out and rebound.
- Break is signaled by a verbal command.
- Player 5 boxes out. Player 3 is to cut to sideline hash mark. Players 2 and 3 can switch responsibilities and the outlet pass can be made on a miss too (diagram 1).
- Player 1 cuts to lower (front court) hash mark to receive pass from player 3 (diagram 1).

Shay Berry
Dartmouth College

Fast Break: Time and Score Quick Step Up (Side)

Diagram 1

Diagram 2

Purpose:

This is a transition offense designed to create a scoring situation for the ballhandler and three-point options for both player 2 and player 4.

Organization:

Player 1 pushes the ball, (player 5 may not be in the play initially), player 2 sets a ball screen creating the drive if two points are needed. If three points are desired, player 4 sets a flare screen for player 2. Player 4 steps to the ball outside of the three-point line (diagram 1).

Variation:

In the event that two points are needed and player 1 gets free off of player 2's screen, player 5 can "seal the help" (diagram 2).

Hot Tips

- This play is most effective when players 2 and 4 are three-point shooters.
- This play requires a point guard (player 1) to read the play and make appropriate decisions depending on the team's needs and personnel in the game.
- The execution and timing of the initial ball screen and flare screen should be drilled often.

Shay Berry
Dartmouth College

Fast Break: Time and Score Quick Step Up (Middle)

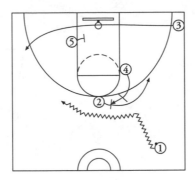

Diagram 1

Purpose:

This is a transition offense designed to create a scoring situation for a three-point shot for both players 2 and 4 with player 3 cutting on the baseline off of player 5's screen.

Organization:

Player 1 advances the ball up the right sideline and crosses over to the left. Player 2 sets a middle pick and flares off of player 4's flare screen. Player 4 steps to the ball after setting the screen. Player 5 sets a baseline screen for player 3 (diagram 1).

- This play is most effective when players 2, 3 and 4 are three-point shooters.
- This play requires a point guard (player 1) to read the play and make appropriate decisions depending on the team's needs and personnel in the game.
- The execution and timing of the initial ball screen and flare screen should be drilled often.
- If the team needs two points, the 3-5 post isolation can be very effective. The lob to player 5 should be available due to the lack of weak-side help.

Shay Berry
Dartmouth College

Fast Break: Time and Score Quick Step Up with Dribble Hand Off

Diagram 1

Diagram 2

Purpose:

This is a transition offense designed to create penetration for the ballhandler (player 2) off of a dribble hand-off that creates options for a lay-up for player 4, penetrate and kick to player 3 and high-low with players 5 and 4.

Diagram 2

Organization:

Player 1 pushes the ball up the left side. Player 2 and player 1 execute a dribble hand-off (diagram 1). Player 4 sets a middle pick and roll for player 2. Player 2 dribbles it to the right side reading the defense and looking to pass to player 3, score on the drive or pass to player 4 in the post, who has rolled off of player 5's backscreen to the right block. Player 5 flashes to the ball for high-low (diagram 2).

Variation:

Player 1 can choose to not execute the dribble hand-off with player 2 and use player 5's ball screen. Player 5 rolls to the basket (diagram 3).

Hot Tips

- This play is most effective when players 1 and 2 have the ability to create penetration. Player 5 is a physical post presence or skilled post player. Player 3 needs to be a perimeter and/or 3-point shooter.
- Player 2 needs to have the experience and decision making skills to read the defense during penetration.
- The execution of player 5's backscreen for player 4 and the time of player 4's cut to the post with player 2's penetration is vital.

Fast Break: Blue Devil

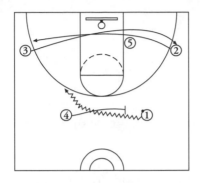

Diagram 1

Diagram 2

Diagram 3

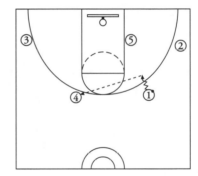

Diagram 4

Diagram 5

Diagram 6

Purpose:

To execute an effective secondary fast break offense that utilizes the trailer as a screener, isolation scorer or a high/low scoring option.

Organization:

Players 2 and 3 will cross in transition. Player 4 comes across and sets a ball screen for 1, who dribbles off to the left (diagram 1). Player 1 reverses the ball to 4, who has cut to replace player 1 at the top of key (diagram 2). Player 4 catches the ball at the top. Player 2 backscreens for 1 (who flares to left wing), and then pops out to top of key. Player 5 backscreens for 3, who cuts from the baseline to the middle of lane. Player 4 looks for 1 on left wing or 3 in middle of lane (diagram 3). Player 1 dribble attacks defender and reverses to 4 (diagram 4). Player 4 catches at top of key, and as defender closes out, player 4 dribble attacks basket (diagram 4).

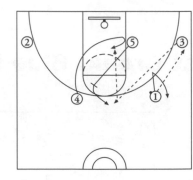

Diagram 7

Variation:

If player 4 is not open for the reversal, 1 passes to 3 on right wing and then makes a v-cut to replace. Player 5 backscreens for 4 (who cuts to right block) and pops out to top of key (diagram 7). Player 3 skip passes to 5 at top, as 4 seals defender, steps in lane, and looks for dump down pass from 5 (diagram 6).

Initial set-up is as follows: Player 1 attacks from the right side of half-court. Player 2 is on the right wing, 3 on the left wing, 5 on the right block, 4 is on the left as trailer of half-court and is the primary ballhandler.

Secondary Offense: UCLA

Diagram 1

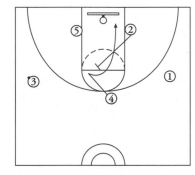

Diagram 2

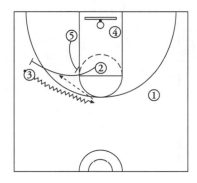

Diagram 3

Diagram 4

Purpose:

To execute an effective man-man offense that utilizes screen the screener out of the secondary break.

Organization:

Player 1 passes to 4, and player 4 reverses to 3. Player 5 flashes across the lane to ballside block. Player 2 cuts to right midblock area (diagram 1). Player 2 now cuts in middle of the lane and moves up to free throw line to set a back screen for player 4 (diagram 2). As player 3 dribbles middle toward the top to create a passing angle, player 5 pops up to middle of ballside post and backscreens for player 2, who cuts over the top to three-point area (diagram 3).

Variation:

The screen on player 2 can be higher and tighter in the lane, 2 will essentially curl cut to the hoop (diagram 3).

- Initial setup is as follows (secondary break): player 3 is on the left wing, 4 is the trailer at the top of the key, player 1 is on the right wing, player 2 in the right corner and player 5 is the right block.

- The screen for player 2 from 5 is a flare screen, where 2 will finish behind the three-point line for a shot (diagram 3).

- Player 3 must dribble to the baseline on 2's curl, so the passing angle can be improved (diagram 4).

Hot Tips

Transition Offense: Shallow

Diagram 1

Diagram 2

Diagram 3

Purpose:

To execute an effective secondary fast break transition offense that culminates into a motion offense.

Organization:

Player 1 dribbles toward player 2 on the right wing. Player 2 uses 4 to make a shallow cut up to replace player 1 at top of key. Players 3 and 5 work to setup next action (diagram 1). Player 1 passes to 2. Player 5 sets a down screen for player 3 who pops to the wing and receives a pass from 2 (diagram 2). Player 3 can shoot or pass to 5 for a quick low post hit (diagram 3).

Variation:

Player 5 screens across for player 4, as player 3 looks into 4. Player 2 screens across for 1. Player 3 reverses the ball to 1 and the offense continues into motion.

Hot Tips

- Initial fast break transition setup is as follows: player 1 starts with the ball at the top of the key (right lane side), player 2 on right wing, player 4 on right block, player 3 is on the left wing and player 5 is trailing the break on left side (lane width).
- Player 1 gives direction with dribble (diagram 1).
- Player 3 dives to left block and player 5 waits to set down screen to set up action for diagram 2.

Transition Offense: Circle

Diagram 1

Diagram 2

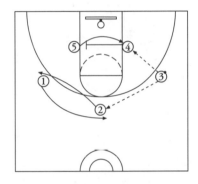

Diagram 3

Purpose:

To execute an effective secondary fast break transition offense that culminates into a motion offense.

Organization:

Player 1 dribbles toward left wing. Player 4 sets a down screen for 2 (on the right block), who pops out to top of key. Player 3 sets up defender for next action, as 5 slides down to elbow/mid-post area from trailer position (diagram 1). Player 1 passes to 2, as player 4 sets another screen for 3, popping out to right wing. Player 2 looks to pass to 3 on right wing (diagram 2). Player 3 can shoot or pass to 4 for a quick low post hit (diagram 3).

Variation:

Player 4 screens across for 5. Player 3 looks into 5, as player 2 interchanges with 1. Player 3 reverses the ball to 1 and the offense continues into motion (diagram 3).

Hot Tips

- Initial fast break transition setup is as follows: player 1 with the ball at top of key (right lane side), player 2 on right wing, player 4 on right block, player 3 left wing and player 5 on left side (lane width outside the 3-point line).
- Player 1 gives direction with dribble (diagram 1).
- As player 1 dribbles toward left wing, 3 dives to left block to set up action for diagram 2.

Transition Offense: Cross

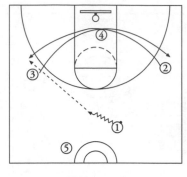

Diagram 1

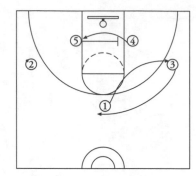

Diagram 2

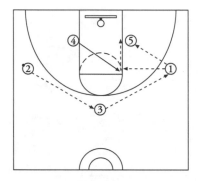

Diagram 3

Purpose:

To execute an effective secondary fast break transition offense that utilizes numerous scoring options and culminates into a motion offense.

Organization:

Player 1 dribbles toward left. On the call from 1, players 2 and 3 cross sides and change wing position. Player 1 passes to 2 (diagram 1). Player 5 has dived from trailer to low ballside block. Player 2 passes to 4 in the low post for an immediate isolation (diagram 2). Player 2 reverses the ball to 3 at the top of key. Player 3 immediately reverses the ball to 1 on the right wing. Player 1 now has a few options (diagram 3).

- Option 1 - Player 1 can pass into player 5 in the low block or execute a pick and roll with 5.
- Option 2 - Player 4 can flash ballside elbow to receive pass from player 1 and execute high/low action with 5.

Variation:

Player 5 screens across for 4. Players 1 and 3 interchange (diagram 2).

Hot Tips

- Player 1 can pass to either 2 or 3 after cross exchange (diagram 1).
- As player 1 dribbles toward left wing, player 5 is trailing, but immediately cuts to left block for next action (diagram 1).

Section Five:
Special Situations

Full-Court: Victory

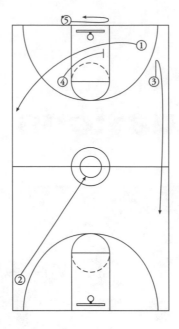

Diagram 1

Purpose:

To execute an effective full-court offensive late game play that exploits three perimeter-scoring opportunities.

Organization:

Player 5 inbounds the ball. Player 4 screens for 1, who cuts across the lane sprinting up the sideline. Player 3 v-cuts toward the ball and goes long up the sideline. Player 2 cuts to the middle of the floor (half-court). Player 5 can pass to 1, 2 or 3. Player 3 looks to score (diagram 1).

- Initial setup is as follows: Player 5 inbounding the ball, 4 is ballside elbow, 3 is opposite ball (right side), 1 is ballside – short corner, and 2 is ballside corner (front-court).
- This play is used to score late in the game with limited time available. If player 5 can run the baseline, 5 must do so to create a better passing angle.

Full-Court: Black

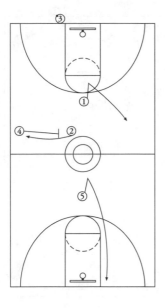

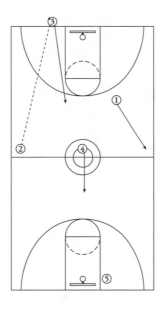

Diagram 1   Diagram 2

Diagram 3

Purpose:

To execute an effective full-court inbounds play with three seconds or more left in the game.

Organization:

Player 3 is the inbounder located on the baseline. Player 2 is at center court and 4 is parallel to him on 3's side of the court. Player 5 is in the front court located directly between the top of the key and center court (diagram 1). Player 2 receives a screen from 4 and cuts to the sideline on 3's side. Player 1 fakes to ball and then v-cuts to opposite side of floor of 2 and should be parallel to 2. Player 3 makes baseball pass to 2. Player 4 runs middle lane and 1 runs outside lane. Player 5 cuts to weakside block corner (diagram 2). Player 2 attacks with dribble. Player 5 has the option of posting up ballside or cutting to the short corner. Player 4 spots up at the top of the key. Player 3 trails and goes to open area. Player 2 reads and makes decision (diagram 3).

- Player 3 is your best passer and is your quarterback. Player 2 should be your best player.
- Players 4 and 5 are your post players, but 4 should be the better shooter.

Full-Court: 14

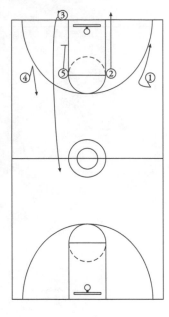

Diagram 1

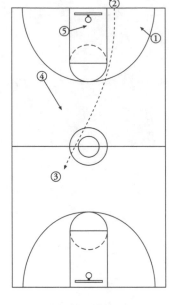

Diagram 2

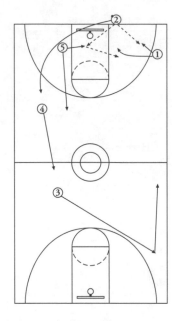

Diagram 3

Purpose:

To execute an effective full-court, inbounds play that will lead to a lay-up. This 1-4 alignment is used if a team can run the baseline and is winning by 1, 2 or 3 points at the end of the game.

Organization:

Option 1 – Player 3 starts with the ball out of bounds and passes it to player 2, who has cut from opposite elbow to out of bounds. Simultaneously, player 4 cuts in from ballside wing toward 3 and then out toward half-court. Player 5 runs down to ballside midpost area to set a backscreen for player 3 who cuts deep for a pass from player 2. Player 1 v-cuts back to player 2 (diagram 1).

Option 1A – Player 2 catches the pass from player 3, and looks to hit 3 deep for a lay-up. Player 5 steps to the ball after backscreen. Player 1 flashes hard toward the ball. Player 4 trails 3 on the play (diagram 2).

Variation:

If player 2 cannot pass to player 3 deep, 2 can pass to player 5 cutting in the lane or to player 1. Either way, get the ball to player 1 and then fill the lanes for the fast break. Player 3 goes to the left side and flashes up, player 4 (trailing) now cuts to the block area, player 2 gets out and fills the right lane and player 5 now becomes the trailer (diagram 3).

- Going from left to right the line is player 1 (opposite of inbounder), player 2 opposite elbow, player 5 ballside elbow and player 4 ballside free throw line extended (outside the 3-point line).
- Player 1 should be your best ballhandler, so if player 3 can't get the pass, player 2 inbounds to 1.
- Don't force it and use players 4 and 1 as relief.

Gary DeCesare
University of Richmond

Full-Court: Touchdown

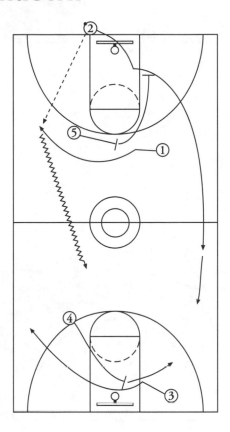

Diagram 1

Purpose:

To execute an effective full-court last second play that has multiple scoring options.

Organization:

Player 5 screens for 1. Player 2 inbounds the ball to 1 and steps in bounds. Player 5 now backscreens for 2 and 2 continues to run down the court (left sideline), as 1 speed dribbles into the frontcourt. Player 4 downscreens for 3, coming off the right side. Player 1 immediately looks for 2, but has 3 as another option

Initial setup is as follows: player 2 inbounds the ball, 5 (ballside) at three-point line in back court, 1 opposite (back court) above three-point line, 4 ballside of front court top of key and player 3 is opposite block in front court.

Full-Court: Final

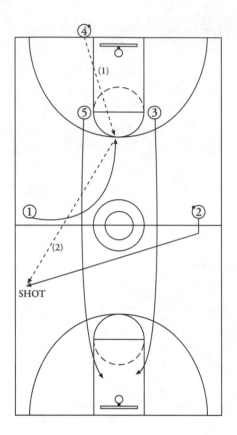

Purpose:
To execute an effective full-court play with under five seconds left in the game.

Organization:
Players 5 and 3 sprint deep to rebound. Player 1 circles through center and tries to receive inbounds pass at top of circle (back court). Player 2 delays a count then sprints to opposite sideline (right) at a diagonal. Player 1 looks for 2, but if no one is open, then 1 dribbles in for shot.

- Initial setup is as follows: player 4 inbounds the ball, 5 (ballside) elbow in back court, 3 opposite elbow in back court, 1 at half-court (back court side), and 2 opposite at half-court (back court side).
- Player 1 is best passer and 2 is best shooter.

Man-Man: Nuggets

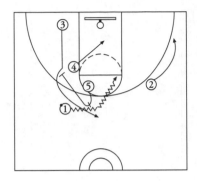

Diagram 1

Purpose:

To execute a man-man quick hitter when you are down 2 points.

Organization:

Player 1 dribbles off a ball screen from player 5, who then sets a down screen for player 3. Player 2 flares to corner as player 1 drives. Player 4 cuts to basket (diagram 1).

- Player 1 looks to drive, draw and dish to player 2 in the corner if 2's defender helps.
- If player 4's defender helps, then 4 has a quick drive to the rim.
- Player 1 can hit player 3 coming off a downscreen at the top for a 3-point shot.

Situation is for being down by two, but if there is a good look at a three-point basket, take it.

Man-Man: Chinle

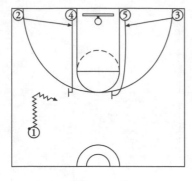

Diagram 1

Diagram 2

Diagram 3

Purpose:

To execute an effective man-man, end of game play out of a 1-4 low alignment that exploits a low post isolation or perimeter jump shot.

Organization:

Play starts in a 1-4 low. Players 4 and 5 flash from blocks to high post elbow. Players 2 and 3 cut from corners to blocks. Player 1 is on left wing (diagram 1). Player 1 comes off of player 4 and 5's stagger double screen and penetrates to the right wing. Player 2 back picks for player 4, who cuts down the lane and comes off another screen from player 3. Player 1 looks for player 4 on ballside block (diagram 2). After screen for player 4, player 3 comes off a stagger double screen from players 2 and 5 to the top of key for 3-point shot (diagram 3).

Variation:

Player 1 can hit player 4 on the block or player 3 at the top (diagram 3).

Player 3 must set a screen in the lane area for player 4 (diagram 2).

Man-Man: Poly Prep

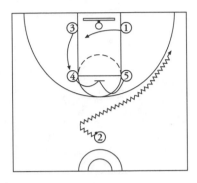

Diagram 1

Diagram 2

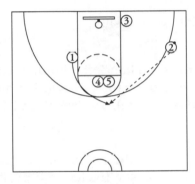

Diagram 3

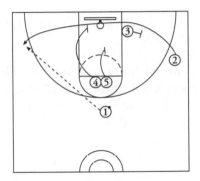

Diagram 4

Purpose:
To execute an end of game, quick hitter against a man-to-man defense that focuses on a quick 2 or 3-point shot.

Organization:
Player 2 starts dribbling away from player 1's side, then dribbles hard below the free throw line on right side (diagram 1). Players 4 and 5 come together at the free throw line. Player 3 tight curls around players 4 and 5 to the right block (diagram 2). Player 1 waits a second for player 3 to come off of players 4 and 5 and then uses their double screen, coming to the top for a three-point shot (diagram 3).

Variations:
- Player 2 turns the corner for a one-on-one move (diagram 1).
- If ball is passed to player 1 and the shot is not available, then player 2 comes off a backscreen set by player 3, and then a stagger double screen set by players 5 and 4 to the left corner (diagram 4).

Hot Tips

- Players 4 and 5 must come as low as possible, but not in the lane (diagram 2).
- Player 2 comes off player 3 at the baseline, player 5 is then higher in the lane and then, finally, player 2 comes off player 4 (diagram 4).
- Teach player 2 the proper footwork for corner catch and shot.

Man-Man: Misdirection #2

Diagram 1

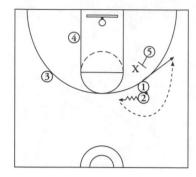

Diagram 2

Purpose:

To execute an effective man-man offense that is used for a last second shot.

Organization:

Player 1 dribbles toward player 2 on the right wing and performs a handoff. Simultaneously, player 3 makes a cut to the basket and comes off 4's down screen to the top of key (diagram 1). Player 5 sets a flare screen for player 1 (pops behind the three-point line), as player 2 quickly turns and passes to 1 for a three-point shot (diagram 2).

Hot Tips

- Initial setup is as follows: Player 1 starts with the ball at the top of the key, player 2 is on the right wing, player 3 is on the left wing, player 4 is in the left mid-post area, and player 5 is in the right mid-post area.

- Player 3 is the decoy in the play, as player 3 comes hard off of 4's screen. Player 2 acts like the pass will go to 3, but must jump stop and reverse the pass. Player 5 lingers around before setting the flare screen (diagram 2).

Man-Man: "3's"

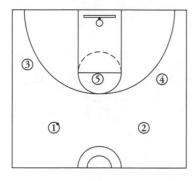

Diagram 1

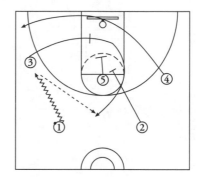

Diagram 2

Purpose:

To execute an effective man-man offense, last second play that results in a 3-point shot.

Organization:

Initial setup is a 2-3 set. Players 1 and 2 are the guards (two guard front), players 3 and 4 are the wings (left and right), and player 5 is in the high post (diagram 1). Player 1 dribbles toward 3 on the left wing. Player 3 leaves the wing and sets a cross screen in the lane for player 4, who cuts hard to ballside corner lane. As player 4 comes off 3's shoulder, players 5 and 2 set a stagger double down screen for 3. Player 3 comes hard off stagger double to top for pass from player 1 and shoot (diagram 2).

- Player 3 must be your best three-point shooter.
- Objective is to get an open three-point shot on the first pass.

Man-Man: Blue

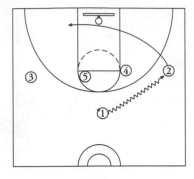

Diagram 1

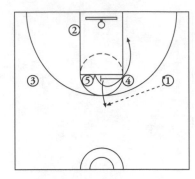

Diagram 2

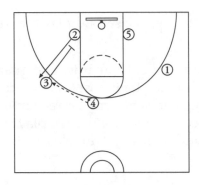

Diagram 3

Purpose:

To execute a man-man set play that is a quick hitter initiated out of the 1-4 high alignment and exploits your best shooter with ten seconds remaining in the half or game.

Organization:

Player 1 dribbles and chases player 2 from the right wing to the left block (diagram 1). Player 4 sets a cross screen for player 5, who cuts to the basket. If player 5 is not open, player 4 rolls to the top for reversal (diagram 2). Player 3 downscreens for player 2, as 2 comes off looking for the shot. Player 4 passes to player 2 on the left wing (diagram 3).

- Run this play with ten seconds left in the quarter or half.
- Player 2 must be you best shooter and player 5 your best post player.
- The set is out of a 1-4 high alignment (diagram 1).
- Player 1 reverses the ball to player 4, if player 5 is not open (diagram 2).

Zone: Double Stack

Diagram 1

Diagram 2

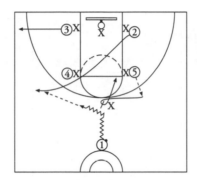

Diagram 3

Purpose:

To execute a set play that is initiated from a box set, useful against any zone defense and ideal for an end of game situation.

Organization:

Player 1 initiates the offense on the side of players 5 and 2 (right). Player 5 pops out and sets a ball screen on player 1's defender. Simultaneously, player 2 makes a diagonal cut to the left wing behind the top guard defender, as player 1 uses the screen from player 5 (diagram 1). Player 1 passes to player 2, as 5 rolls. Player 4 pins zone defender (back forward) as player 3 pops to left ballside corner (diagram 2).

Variations:

- Versus Odd Front Zone: Player 2 must read the forward defender on left side and look for player 4 on the post-pin or player 3 on the pop out to ballside corner (diagram 3).
- Versus Even Front Zone: Player 2 might get an open look for a shot, or look to player 4 on the post-pin, player 3 popping out or player 5 rolling after high post ball-screen.

Hot Tip

Offense must be adjusted to the front but effective versus odd/even front of zone.

Zone: Blue Devil

Diagram 1

Diagram 2

Diagram 3

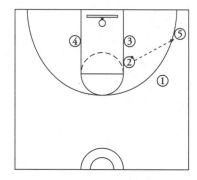

Diagram 4

Purpose:

To execute an end of game, quick hitter against a zone defense.

Organization:

Player 5 passes to player 1 on the right wing, as player 2 cuts to the right corner. Player 4 screens the bottom of the zone. As player 2 gets under the basket, player 5 cuts down the middle (diagram 1). Player 1 passes to player 2 in the right corner as player 5 comes to the block, receiving a screen from player 3 (diagram 2). Player 2 drives left toward the gap in the middle. Player 5 releases to the corner spotting up behind the 3-point line (diagram 3). Player 2 stops hard and kicks the ball to player 5 for a 3-point shot (diagram 4).

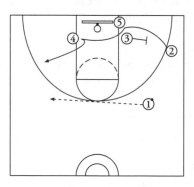

Diagram 5

Variations:

- Player 2 turns the corner for a one-on-one move (diagram 1).
- If ball is passed to player 1 and the shot is not available, then player 2 comes off a back screen set by player 3, and then a stagger double screen set by players 5 and 4 to the left corner (diagram 5).

Special Situations

- Player 2 must drive hard, protecting the ball, split the gap and draw the defense (diagram 3).
- Player 5 must watch player 2 as the drive is made toward the middle, so player 5 can time the set up for a shot in the corner.

Zone: Sweep

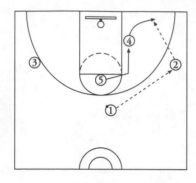

Diagram 1

Diagram 2

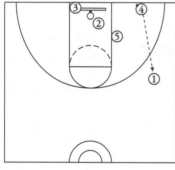

Diagram 3

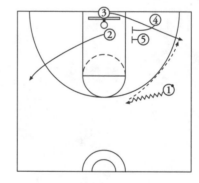

Diagram 4

Purpose:

To create an open three-point shot at the end of the half verses a zone.

Organization:

Player 1 passes to player 2 on the right wing, simultaneously player 4 steps out to the short corner. Player 5 follows the pass and flashes to the mid-post area where 4 began (diagram 1). Player 4 receives the pass in the short corner from player 2, who immediately cuts through the lane. Player 3 begins to make a baseline cut from the weak side. Player 1 flashes to right sideline (diagram 2). Player 4 reverses the ball to player 1, as 2 and 3 are bypassing each other around the basket (diagram 3). Player 1 dribbles left toward the top of key and is looking (decoy) at player 2 cutting to the left side 3-point line. Player 4 steps back to post and sets a double screen with player 5 for 3, coming to the corner. Player 1 looks for either player 2 or 3, but 3 is open most often.

Hot Tips

- Initiate the play with 14 seconds on the clock, and it will result in a shot at the buzzer.
- Players begin in a 1-3-1 set with player 1 at top, player 3 at the left wing, 2 at the right wing, player 5 at the free throw line and player 4 at the right midpost area. The best passer needs to be in low mid post.
- Very good set for a 3-point shot attempt at the end of the half.
- Works best against a zone defense, but can be effective verses a man-man.
- Can be a continuity offense if needed.

Out of Bounds: Low Shot Clock

Diagram 1

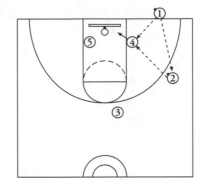

Diagram 2

Purpose:

To execute an effective baseline out of bounds play that is executed with little time on the shot clock. This play utilizes screening and cutting action to free up a perimeter shooter.

Organization:

Player 3 backscreens for 5, (who cuts from ballside elbow to opposite block) and then pops out to top of key. Player 4 cuts toward ball, down screens for 2, (who cuts in toward baseline and then to the right sideline wing) and dives toward ballside block. Player 1 passes to 2, looking for the shot (diagram 1).

Variation:

Player 1 passes to 2 for the shot (diagram 2), or
- 2 can pass to 4 for low post score.
- 1 can pass to 4, who slips into the lane after screen for 2.

Hot Tips

- Initial setup is as follows: player 1 inbounds the ball, 2 is ballside corner, 3 is opposite block, and players 4 and 5 are stacked ballside elbow.
- Player 2 must fake the cut is baseline toward the basket, so the defense can be set up for a flare screen off of 4 (diagram 1).
- Player 4 must set a good screen for 2, then quickly release to the basket, looking for pass from (diagram 1).

Mike Granato
Weir High School

Out of Bounds: 4-Across

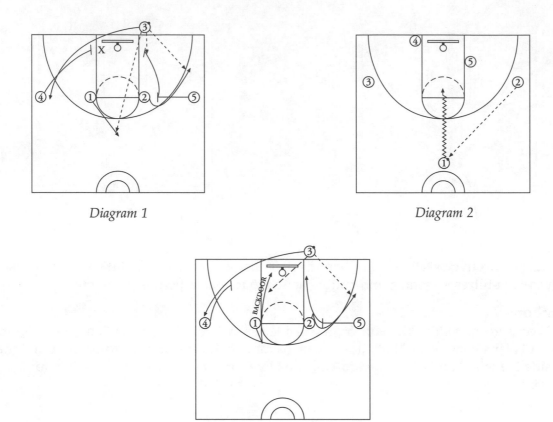

Diagram 1

Diagram 2

Diagram 3

Purpose:

To execute a baseline out of bounds play against man, zone or combo, that is initiated out of a 1-4 high alignment and effective for late in the game situations.

Organization:

Option 1: vs Zone/Combo – On the slap of ball, player 3 looks to pass to player 2 (who is coming off of player 5's cross screen) to ballside corner looking for a jump shot. After screening for player 2, player 5 then dives in the lane and looks for pass from player 3. Player 1 pops out to top of key for defensive balance or outlet pass. Player 4 sprints down to baseline to set a back screen on forward defender for player 3 (inbound passer) cutting off to opposite wing after inbounding the ball to player 2. Player 4 then steps to opposite block (diagram 1). If player 2 does not take the shot, then the ball is reversed to player 1 at the top of key and 1 dribble penetrates to the middle of the zone looking for the posts and wings (diagram 2).

Variations:

Same action as option 1, but vs Man, the weakside players 4 and 1 may utilize backdoor cuts to get open for a lay-up (diagram 3).

Out of Bounds: Sideline Box

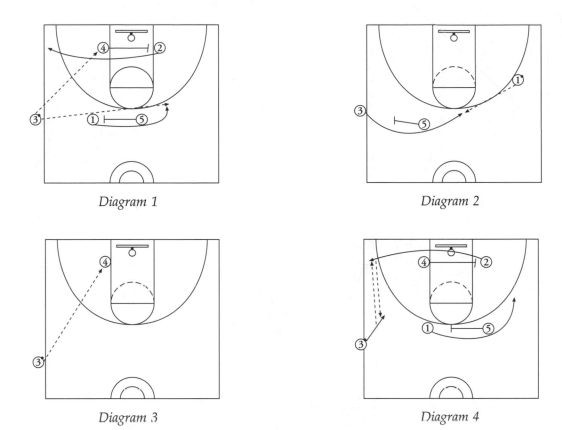

Diagram 1

Diagram 2

Diagram 3

Diagram 4

Purpose:

To execute a sideline out of bounds play that is a quick hitter. Best utilized after a time out (usually at the end of the game).

Organization:

Player 5 sets a backscreen for the player 1. If player 1 is open and receives the pass from player 3, player 1 has room to execute a one on one move to score. Simultaneously, player 2 runs off a cross screen set by player 4 to the ballside corner for a potential jump shot (diagram 1).

Variations:

- If player 1 can't score, then 1 executes a dribble drive to the right wing, as player 5 sets a back screen for player 3 (inbounder). Player 1 can pass back to player 3 for a foul line jump shot (diagram 2).

- Player 3 makes the inbounds pass to player 4, who has posted up on the ballside low block after cross screen for player 2 (diagram 3).

- The "box special" should be used with 3-5 seconds on the game clock. The first pass goes to player 2, who immediately passes back to player 3 (the inbounder) for a quick three-point shot (diagram 4).

Out of Bounds: Game Winner

Diagram 1

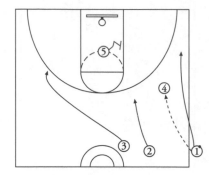

Diagram 2

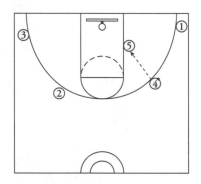

Diagram 3

Purpose:

To execute an end of game sideline out of bounds play.

Organization:

Player 3 screens for player 2 or vice versa (decoy). Player 5 v-cuts hard and then screens in the middle for player 4. Player 4 flashes to the ball (diagram 1). Player 1 passes to player 4, who flashed outside the 3-point line to receive the ball. Player 5 then seals, as player 3 fills the left wing to corner, player 2 goes to the left top of key and player 1 to the right sideline to corner (diagram 2). Player 4 passes to player 5, and 5 makes the read, either to score or hit offside guards 2 or 3 (diagram 3).

Hot Tips

- Player 1 takes the ball out, as players 2 and 3 set up side by side at half-court. Player 4 sets up opposite block, as player 5 starts on ballside block.
- After player 4 receives the pass from player 1, the cuts from 1, 2 and 3 must be hard and spaced to present scoring opportunities.

Shay Berry
Dartmouth College

Out of Bounds: Post and Cut

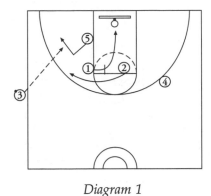

Diagram 1

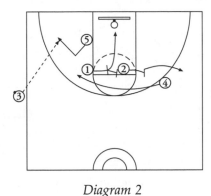

Diagram 2

Diagram 3

Purpose:

Side out of bounds play designed to get a lay-up with less than four seconds left on the clock.

Organization:

Player 3 takes it out on the sideline (best if about three steps above the foul line). Player 5 cuts to wing inside of the three-point line. Player 3 inbounds the ball to 5. Player 1 cross screens for player 2, 2 cuts to left elbow, player 1 dives to the basket. Player 4 is spotted in the right slot (diagram 1).

Variation:

- All players are aligned like the above play. Player 3 inbounds the ball to player 5. Players 1 and 2 cross screen for 4, 2 steps out to the right slot and player 1 dives to the basket (diagram 3).

- Player 3 passes directly to player 4 off of the double screen from players 1 and 2 (diagram 3).

- This play is most effective when player 4 is a shooter. This will freeze the help defense and open the lane up for player 1 to dive to the basket.
- If player 1 is not open, 2 should be free for the open elbow jumper.
- A direct pass to player 4 is an option if they sag in the paint.

Out of Bounds: Post and Cross

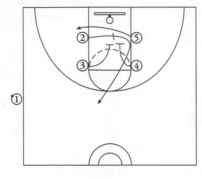

Diagram 1

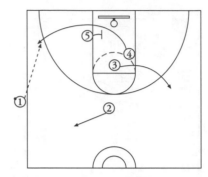

Diagram 2

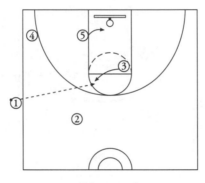

Diagram 3

Purpose:

Side out of bounds play designed with options to get a lay-up to player 5 and shot from player 2. Used when there are more than five seconds on the clock.

Organization:

Player 1 takes the ball out of bounds. The players line up in a box. Player 2 cross screens for 5, players 3 and 4 double screen for 2 (this action is an option but is mostly used as a decoy). This part of the play must move quickly, even if movement starts before the ball is handed to the inbounder. After the screen the screener action, player 4 cuts of 5's screen to the left corner. Player 3 gets out to the right slot. Player 5 seals the defender. Player 4 throws lob pass to 5 (diagrams 1 and 2).

Variation:

If player 4 is covered, 3 can flash back to the ball, receive the pass and 3 can pass to the post or wing (diagram 3).

Hot Tips

- Player 5 must do a great job of sealing or none of the lob options become available.
- The inbounder needs to let the lob play develop.
- It is important for player 2 to be a decoy, because it will spread the defense and let the high-lows develop.
- This play can also be effective against a zone defense.

Delay Game: Marquette

Diagram 1

Diagram 2

Diagram 3

Diagram 4

Purpose:

To execute an effective half-court, delay of game play that will lead to a lay-up. This traingle aligned delay game utilizes screens and back door cuts.

Organization:

Option 1 – Player 3 starts at the free throw line in the high post. Players 1 and 2 start wide. Player 3 passes to player 1 then down screens for 3, who pops out to the top (diagram 1). Player 2 immediately passes to player 3, pops out and then downscreens for 1 at the free throw line (diagram 2).

Option 2: 88 – Player 1 passes to player 2 (as in Marquette) and then receives a backscreen from player 3 for a lay-up. Player 2 hits 1 with a pass and score (diagram 5).

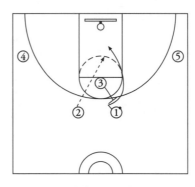

Diagram 5

Variations:

- Player 5 flashes up to receive pass from player 1, who immediately downscreens for player 3 (diagram 3).
- Player 3 receives the pass from player 5, immediately reverses the ball to player 2, and then screens down for player 1, which continues the Marquette play (diagram 4).

- Players 1, 2 and 3 must be your best ballhandlers.
- Players 4 and 5 must stay wide and flash hard up their respective sidelines for a decoy pass or relief.
- While in the triangle (at the very top), if any player (1, 2 or 3) cannot make the pass to the opposite (top) guard, then player 4 or 5 would flash up on the respective side to receive the pass. The guard who made the pass would then down screen for the post guard.
- Option 2: 88 – This is predicated on the call of the guard with the ball, usually with a few seconds of the shot clock and after Marquette has been run for some time (diagram 5).

Corner

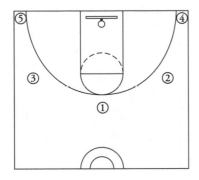

Diagram 1

Diagram 2

Purpose:

To execute an effective man-man offense that initiates from an open set with no post players. Perfect play to use on a deadball possession, after a timeout or free throw attempt.

Organization:

All players are on the perimeter. Player 1 is at the top, players 2 and 3 are on the wings and 4 and 5 are in the corners (diagram 1). Player 1 dribbles to the right wing. Player 3 goes down to set the first part of the stagger double screen for 5. Player 2 back cuts to the middle for the second part of the stagger double screen for 5. Player 4 v-cuts and will come off ballscreen with 1. Player 5 comes to foul line area off a stagger double screen from players 3 and 2, looking for the pass from 1 (diagram 2).

Variation:

If a three-point shot is needed, player 5 pops out to the top of key in the three-point area (diagram 2).

 Hot Tip Initial setup is as follows: player 1 at top, players 5 and 4 are on the left and right elbow, respectively, and players 3 and 2 are on the left and right block, respectively.

Point

Purpose:

To execute an effective man-man offense that initiates from an open set and isolates a shot for the point guard. Perfect play to use on a deadball possession, after a timeout or free throw attempt.

Organization:

All players are on the perimeter. Player 1 is at the top, players 2 and 3 are on the wings, and players 4 and 5 in the corners. Player 1 passes to 2 on the right wing and screens away for 3. Player 3 comes off player 1 for a basket cut, but instead of continuing, 3 turns back and rescreens for 1. Player 1 comes back to free throw line area.

Variation:

If a three-point shot is needed, then player 1 pops out to the top of key in the three-point area.

 Initial setup is as follows: player 1 at top, players 5 and 4 are on the left and right elbow, respectively, and players 3 and 2 are on the left and right block, respectively.

Shay Berry
Dartmouth College

Quick Score: Jump Ball

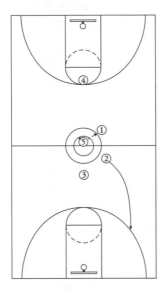

Diagram 1

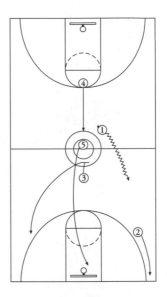

Diagram 2

Purpose:

This jump ball play is designed to create an aggressive game plan and score on the initial jump ball.

Organization:

Player 1 aligns right or left of the circle depending on the jump center's strong hand. In diagram 1, player 1 will align to the right. Player 3 is placed one step off of the jump circle in front of the centers. Player 4 is at the defense foul line for defensive balance. Player 2 aligns at half-court on the right side. Player 5 tips to 1, 2 runs ahead. Player 3 sets a backscreen for 5 and fills the opposite lane. Player 4 trails the play. Player 5 receives the backscreen and sprints to the front of the rim looking for a lob pass for the lay-up or dunk. If player 5 is not open, 1 can throw it ahead to player 2 and 2 can make a post to 5 on the post up. If player 5 is not an option, 1 or 2 can reverse the ball through 4, as the players will be aligned with player 4 out and player 1 in (diagram 2).

Hot Tips

- This play is best effective when practiced often.
- Player 5 should be an athletic center that can run.
- The element of surprise will allow the center to be wide open.
- The point guard must not have fear to throw the lob or throw it ahead to player 2.

Glossary of Terms

For most of our readers, this glossary might seem redundant. However, we realize that some of you might be neophytes to the world of coaching basketball. For this group, we created this list of definitions. Please note that coaches may use different terms to express the same concepts or use one term to express different ideas. To say the least, the vernacular of basketball is not a precise science. With this in mind, we offer you this glossary in order to clear up some of the confusion.

2-Man Game: When two players in any offensive scheme work with each other. One of these players must have the ball. An example of some of the options here are "pick and roll" and "pick and pop." In the former, a screen is set for the dribbler and the screener cuts to the basket. In the latter, the screener moves to the perimeter.

3-Out 2-In Motion: An offensive with three perimeter players and two post players. They can move as two different units (i.e., post with post players and perimeter with perimeter players) or all together.

4-Man Motion: An offensive set in which four players move around a single post player. The post player can be high, low, or move between the two areas.

4-Out Motion: See 4-Man motion above.

5-Out Set: An offensive set in which all five players are located on the perimeter.

Attack Area: Any area in the front court in which an offense can initiate its movement.

Back Pick: Another expression for a "back screen."

Backup Dribble: An offensive movement in which the dribbler moves away from the basket while still facing it. This movement creates space for the offensive player while achieving offensive balance.

Ball Screen: Any screen that is set for the player with the ball.

Banana Cut: A movement by an offensive player without the ball where he curves to get open. Similar to the "loop" and not as tight as a "curl cut."

Basket Cut: A movement by an offensive player without the ball in which he cuts directly to the basket.

Box Set: An offensive set that resembles a box, with two players on the elbows and two players on the blocks. The point guard is usually located at the top of the key when the offense is originally initiated.

Butt Screen: A screen by the high post player for any offensive player who cuts off of him. This can be performed even when the high post player has possession of the ball.

Close Out: A movement in which the defender attempts to quickly get to an offensive player that he has played off of and has just received the ball.

Combo Defense: Any defense that combines elements of two other defenses, e.g., a "box-and-one" or a "triangle-and-two."

Continuity Offense: An offense in which the movement of all the players will result in the players ending up at their original starting positions.

Curl Cut: A movement by an offensive player without the ball in which he tightly curves to get open. This cut can be used with a screen.

Cut and Replace: When an offensive player moves into an area that has just been vacated by a cutter.

Cut Off Player: When two offensive players without the ball move past each other, usually shoulder-to-shoulder, to get open. This is done by a movement generally known as a "brush cut."

Deadball Possession: Any offensive possession immediately after a clock stoppage, e.g., violation, fouls, out of bounds.

Decoy: Any offensive player who is used to deceive the defense by creating the perception that he is the focus of the offense's attention.

Distorting the Zone: When the initial alignment of a zone defense breaks down by the successful movement of both players and ball by the offense.

Dive: A movement by an offensive player without the ball in which he cuts directly to the basket. Similar to a "basket cut."

Double Down: A defensive tactic that counters any post entry. After the offense has entered the ball into the post, a defensive player from the perimeter will leave his assigned man and help defend the post.

Double Screen: When two offensive players set a screen together in tandem. When this type of screen is set in the block area it is know as a "stack."

Double Staggered Screen: When an offensive player uses two separate screens in a row to get open.

Dribble Attack: When the dribbler brings the ball to an area in the front court to initiate the offense. The area that he dribbles to is known as the "attack area."

Dribble Chase: When the offensive player dribbles at his teammate forcing him to vacate the area. The cutter either "basket cuts" or "shallow cuts." This movement can be part of a "dribble attack" in order to initiate the offense.

Dribble Drive: When the offensive player attempts to reach the basket by the use of his dribble.

Dribble Handoff: An offensive movement in which the ball handler dribbles at his teammate and then hands off the ball to him. This movement creates a screening effect.

Duck In: An offensive movement in which the player locates himself in the post in a position where the offense can pass the ball to him.

Dump Down: A pass from the perimeter to the low post. Also known as a "post entry."

Elbow High: An offensive area located halfway between the ten-second line (i.e. half court line) and the elbow.

Face Cut: A movement by an offensive player without the ball in which he cuts directly to the basket. Before he makes this move, the cutter steps at the defender to move him away from his path to the basket.

Fade Screen: Similar to a "flare screen."

Glossary of Terms

Fill In: When an offensive player without the ball moves into an area that has just been vacated by another offensive player. This movement will "balance" the offense.

Flare Cut: A movement by an offensive player without the ball in which he cuts away from the ball handler. A "flare or fade screen" is usually used with this cut. The "skip pass" is also used to get the ball to the cutter.

Flare Screen: A screen set to get a player open on a "flare cut." The screener is facing the ball handler. Usually the defender covering the cutter is paying attention to the dribbler and does not see the screen.

Flex Cut: A "back screen" set along the baseline for a cutter. This screen is the primary screen in the "Flex Offense."

Flex Offense: A "continuity offense" based on the "flex screen" and a down screen.

Fluff Screen: When an offensive player fakes setting a screen to distract the defense. The quasi-screener is being used as a "decoy."

High/Low Action: An offensive scheme that involves both a low and high post.

J-Cut: A movement by an offensive player without the ball in which he tightly curves to get open. This cut can be used with a screen. Similar to the "curl cut."

Kick the Ball: When the dribbler penetrates the defense in order to make the defenders converge on him and leave their defensive assignments. The dribbler can pass the ball to the now open perimeter players for a jump shot. This is an effective tactic against zone defenses.

L-Cut: A movement by an offensive player without the ball in which he cuts on a 90° angle. This cut can be used with a screen.

L-Screen: A screen by an offensive player in which his movement resembles an L. The screener changes direction 90°.

Loop Cut: A movement by an offensive player without the ball where he curves to get open. Similar to the "banana cut " and not as tight as a "curl cut."

Pick and Pitch: A movement by an offensive player without the ball in which he cuts off the high post using the post player as a screen. The post player can pitch the ball back to the cutter.

Screen the Screener: Any screening action in which the screener on a given play will receive a screen after the first screen has been set.

Seal: An action by an offensive player in which he attempts to block a defensive player from the ball. This can be done in the post for a "dump down" or after setting a screen. Sometimes the screener will deliberately let the defender go by him, e.g., "slip by."

Seal the Help: When the offensive player blocks a potential weakside defender from helping his teammate who is defending the ball.

Secondary Break: An option by the offense when the fast break is stopped. By using the players that were not part of the initial fast break, i.e., "trailers," the offense can run a set play off the fast break.

Sell the Play: When an offensive player successfully misdirects the defense into believing that the offensive is doing something different.

Shallow Cut: A movement by an offensive player without the ball when the dribbler performs a "dribble chase." The cutter curves underneath the dribbler and replaces him in the spot the dribbler just vacated. The shallow cut is similar to the "curl cut."

Shape Up To the Ball: The posture of a player's body as he prepares to receive a pass from his teammate. The receiver's body language tells his teammate that he is ready. The receiver's body is in a position to quickly enter the "triple threat position."

Short Corner: An area located halfway between the sideline and the block along the baseline.

Shuffle Cut: A movement by an offensive player without the ball in which he cuts off the high post. The cutter attempts to go over the screen on the side of the passer. The screen used in this movement is known as a "slice screen." This cut is the main focus of a "continuity offense" known as the "Shuffle Offense."

Slice Screen: A back screen that is used by the high post for the player that is performing a "shuffle cut."

Slipping the Screen: When the defense overplays the offensive player receiving a screen, the screener can go under the defense and cut to the basket.

Slip By: When the screener in a zone offense deliberately lets the defensive player he has just screened go by to create his own scoring opportunity by opening up a passing lane between himself and his teammate with the ball.

Skip Pass: A pass that is thrown from one side of the court to the other. The pass must go over or "skip" over the defense.

Spin and Pin: An offensive movement in which the post player seals the defender by use of a reverse pivot.

Spin and Seal: Same as Spin and Seal above.

Staggered Double Screen: Same as Double Staggered Screen above.

Stretch the Zone: When the zone defense extends itself too far by both player and ball movement of an effective zone offense.

Touch and Go: A screening action in which both the screener and the receiver of the screen move quickly to their next spot as soon as the screen is set.

Trailer: Any offensive player that follows the fast break up the court. This player is an important component in the "secondary break."

Triangle Alignment: When three offensive players are aligned so that there are passing lanes between all three players.

Triple Staggered Screen: When an offensive player uses three separate screens in a row to get open.

Triple Threat: The initial position of a player's body after he has received the ball. From this position the player can shoot, pass, or dribble.

Walk Away Screen: When the screener on a pick and roll sets another screen for an offensive player away from the ball. He does this as he rolls away from the pick and roll.

Wheel: A "continuity offense" predicated on the "shuffle cut." Similar to the "Shuffle Offense."

Widens Out: When an offensive player squares up to the basket after receiving the ball or shapes up to the passer in anticipation of receiving the ball. In either case, the player is in an athletic posture ready to shot the ball.

Wideouts: In a 1-4 pressbreaker set, the two outside players. They are aligned on both the left and right sides of foul line extended.

X-Cut: When two offensive players without the ball cross each other's path when they cut. The shape of their two cuts resembles an X.

Zipper Cut: A movement by an offensive player without the ball where he moves straight up (zipper up) or down (zipper down), perpendicular to the baseline. The cut is done in the three-second area. Similar to the "loop" and not as tight as a "curl cut."

Zone Overload: This is one method of "distorting a zone." By flooding an area with offensive players, the defense will have to adjust and change its alignment.

Coach Biographies

Bill Ackerman is the head boy's coach at West York Senior High School in York, Pennsylvania. In addition, Ackerman is a counselor at the Five-Star Basketball Camp and at Michigan State's Basketball Camp.

Jason Adkins is currently the head boy's basketball coach at Colerain High School in Cincinnati, Ohio, where he also teaches in the Social Studies Department. Adkins is the former men's basketball manager at Miami University (Ohio) and head boy's coach at Kings High School.

Mike Batell is currently the video coordinator at Duke University. Prior to Duke, Batell was the youngest head boy's varsity coach in America. He was only 19 when he became the varsity mentor at Drew Prep School in California. Batell has worked numerous sessions at Five-Star.

Tony Bergeron is the full-time recruiting coordinator for the Five-Star Basketball Camp. Prior to Five-Star, Bergeron served as head coach at the MacDuffie School in Springfield, Massachusetts, where he led them to a NEPSAC Championship. Currently, Coach Bergeron is the head boy's coach at the Wings Academy in the Bronx, New York, and has led them to PSAL B-Division Finals in just one season.

Neil Berkman is beginning his first season as head boy's basketball coach at Archbishop Curley High School in Baltimore, Maryland. Berkman is the former assistant men's coach at Siena College, Cornell University, as well as administrative assistant men's coach at Coastal Carolina University. Berkman is a veteran Five-Star Basketball Camp staff member.

Shay Berry's name is synonymous with Five-Star Basketball Camp. Recently named assistant caoch at Dartmouth College, Berry recently served as the camp's marketing director. He has been an assistant coach at Central State University in Ohio, Yale University, Fordham University and New York University. Berry's coaching expertise reaches well beyond the United States borders as he has coached in Russia, the Dominican Republic, Portugal and Spain.

Scott Bogumil is the head boy's coach at Libertyville High School in Illinois. He was previously at Gordon Tech in Chicago, where he was named Illinois District Coach of the Year in 1998 and 2000. Bogumil has been with Five-Star for the past 12 years. Since 1997, he has been the commissioner of the famous Five-Star Development League.

Mark Bollinger is the head boy's coach at River Valley High School in Marion, Ohio. Besides working at Five-Star, Mark has been a staff member at the Ohio State, Kentucky, Duke, and Notre Dame basketball camps.

Mike Brey is the head men's coach for the University of Notre Dame. Prior to Notre Dame, Brey spent eight seasons as an assistant coach at Duke University and is the former head coach at the University of Delaware.

Barry Brodzinski is the head boys' basketball coach at Paul VI High School in New Jersey. Brodzinski is a Five-Star veteran of over 20 years and has successfully coached at both the high school and collegiate levels.

John Calipari is the head coach for the University of Memphis. He has also been the head coach of the University of Massachusetts and the New Jersey Nets. On June 16, 2002, Coach Cal was inducted into the Five-Star Basketball Camp Hall of Fame.

Brad Campbell is currently the head boy's basketball coach at Cinnaminson High School in Cinnaminson, New Jersey. Campbell is the former boy's head coach at Pequannock High School (NJ) and has also served as a college men's assistant coach at Washington College and Salisbury University.

Pete Cinella is in his 10th year as the women's basketball coach at the American International College in Springfield, Massachusetts. While at the AIC, Cinella has led his Yellow Jackets to their best season record (28-4) in school history, advancing to the NCAA Division II Elite Eight in 2002.

Greg Collins is in his second year as the assistant women's coach at the University of Louisville. His coaching expertise includes serving as an assistant athletic director, junior varsity head coach, and assistant varsity coach at DuPont Manual High School in Louisville.

Steve Culp is an assistant boy's basketball coach for the famed St.Vincent-St. Mary High School in Akron, Ohio, where he helped Lebron James develop his game. Prior to St.Vincent-St. Mary, Culp was the former boy's head coach of Akron Firestone High School and assistant men's coach at University of Akron. He is also an 11-year Five-Star Basketball Camp veteran.

Paul Culpo is the head men's coach at Hartwick College in Oneonta, New York. Culpo has also been the head coach of the Doncaster Panthers of the National Basketball League in England and assistant coach at the University of Massachusetts.

Chris Cundiff is the head boy's varsity coach at Carroll Kuemper High School in Carroll, Iowa. He is also the former head coach of Dallas-Center Grimes High School in Iowa. Cundiff has been with Five-Star since 1998.

Mike Daley is the head men's basketball coach at Nazareth College in Rochester, New York. Daley has coached high school basketball in Ohio for 14 years and has served as an assistant at Niagara University.

Gary DeCesare is in his second year as assistant men's basketball coach at the University of Richmond in Richmond, Virginia. Prior to this, DeCesare was the head boy's coach at the legendary St. Raymond's High School in the Bronx, New York. While at St. Raymond's, DeCesare was named New York State Coach of the Year on three occasions (1987, 1991 and 2001) and Kodak Boy's Coach of the Year in 1993. He has also served as the Director of the Adidas Basketball Camp (ABCD) since 1993.

Lee DeForest recently accepted a position with the Central Florida Community College's coaching staff. Previously, he was the assistant men's coach at Bellarmine University in Louisville, Kentucky. DeForest began his coaching career as student-assistant at Eastern Kentucky University in Richmond, Kentucky. He then served as both varsity assistant and head junior varsity coach at Clinton County High School in Clinton, Kentucky.

Kenny Edwards is currently the head boy's basketball coach at Princess Anne High School in Virginia. Prior to this, Kenny was the former head boy's coach at Cox High School in Virginia Beach for 11 years. Overall, he has won three district titles and has had 12 articles published in national basketball magazines.

Mike Feagans is currently the head boy's basketball coach at Rensselaer Central High School, Rensselaer, Indiana. Mike spends his summer time coaching at Five-Star Basketball Camp, where he is 4-year veteran.

Coach Biographies

Matt Fine is in his fifth year as boy's varsity assistant at Muncie Central High School in Muncie, Indiana. Prior to Muncie Central, Fine was an assistant at Winchester High School in Winchester, Indiana, for five years.

Fran Fraschilla is currently employed as an ESPN college basketball analyst. His coaching résumé includes head men's coaching jobs at the University of New Mexico, St. John's University and Manhattan College.

Cory Furman begins his third year as the head men's assistant at Goshen College in Goshen, Indiana. Prior to arriving at Goshen, Furman was an assistant men's coach at Luther College in Decorah, Iowa.

Daryn Freedman is the head boy's basketball coach at Brimmer and May School in Chestnut Hill, Massachusetts. He has spent the past seven summers honing his coaching skills at the Five-Star Basketball Camp and began his coaching career working under Coach John Calipari at the University of Massachusetts.

Tim Goodwin has established the Master's School in West Simsbury, Connecticut, as a New England Prep power. He has shared his expertise at the Five-Star Basketball Camp for the past 12 years.

Mike Granato is the current head basketball coach at Weir Senior High School in Weirton, West Virginia, and has been working with Five-Star for the past three summers.

John Grant has been involved with basketball for 25 years. He has coached at the Youth Olympic level in Scotland and founded the Arbroath Musketeers. Currently he is the head boy's coach at Arbroath High School in Scotland.

Billy Hahn is the head men's coach at LaSalle University. Hahn has been the head coach at Ohio University, the University of Rhode Island, and at Morris Harvey College in West Virginia. Hahn earned his solid recruiting reputation while serving as an assistant at the University of Maryland.

Keith Holubesko is the current head varsity boy's coach at Case High School in Swansea, Massachusetts. Keith has been a part of Five-Star Basketball Camp for the past six year, working for both the girl's and boy's camps as a stationmaster and league commissioner. Holubesko is the former women's assistant basketball coach at Bridgewater State College in Massachusetts and head girl's basketball coach at Rogers High School in Newport, Rhode Island.

Everett Jackson is in his second year as assistant coach at the University South Alabama. E.J. is the former head girl's coach at Deerfield Beach High School, Deerfield Beach, Florida, where he led his team to two state final four appearances in four seasons. He has also served as a camp instructor at the Five-Star Women's Basketball Camp.

Stan Jones is currently in his second season as the associate men's basketball coach at Florida State University. Jones rejoined Coach Lenoard Hamilton's staff after spending a year as the assistant men's coach at Mississippi State University. Prior to the 2001-2002 season, Jones served as Coach Hamilton's assistant with the Washington Wizards of the NBA and the University of Miami (Florida).

John Jungers is currently the assistant men's coach at Iowa Western Community College in Council Bluffs, Iowa. Jungers, a former Texas A&M player, was also the top assistant men's coach at NAIA power Bellevue University in Bellevue, Nebraska.

Kerry Keating is an assistant men's basketball coach at UCLA. Prior to this position with the Bruins, Keating served as an assistant coach at the University of Tennessee, Appalachian State, and Seton Hall University.

Dan Kiser is the former assistant men's basketball coach at Framingham State College in Framingham, Massachusetts. Prior to coaching for the Rams, Kiser was an assistant coach with

Endicott College and is also the former head coach at Eastern Nazarene College. Kiser is well known in the Five-Star family. He has worked various sessions, serving as a stationmaster, league commissioner, and resident coach for the past five summers.

Mike Krzyzewski is in his 24th season as head men's coach at Duke University. Coach K has led the Blue Devils to three NCAA National Championships (1992, 1993 and 2001), while being named National Coach of the Year 12 times. He was inducted to the Naismith Memorial Basketball Hall of Fame in 2001.

Chris Kusnerick is beginning his third year at Rock Falls High School in Illinois. Previously, Kusnerick coached at St. Anthony High School in Effingham, Illinois, and Perryville High School in Perryville, Missouri.

Stu Lash is the scouting coordinator for the Denver Nuggets and credits all his success to Five-Star Basketball Camp, where he was the recruiting coordinator and marketing director. He also served as an assistant coach to the Five-Star Hawks. Prior to Five-Star, Lash was a manager for the men's basketball team at the University of Massachusetts under Coach John Calipari.

Douglas Leichner is the head boy's varsity basketball coach at Osceola High School in Kissimee, Florida. Prior to Osceola, Leichner was head coach at Merritt Island High School in Merritt Island, Florida, as well as Episopal High School in Jacksonville, Florida.

Jessica Mannetti is the head girls' varsity coach at Greens Farms Academy in Greens Farms, Connecticut. Mannetti is the former director of devolvement for the Five-Star Women's Basketball Camp. She played an instrumental role in developing the partnership between the Five-Star Women's Basketball Camp and such WNBA stars as Tamika Catchings, Stepahnie White, Katie Douglas and Nykesha Sales.

Matt Masiero has been the Director of the Five-Star Women's Basketball Camp since 1998 and has worked for the Five-Star Basketball Camp for the past 11 years. He recently co-edited the *Five-Star Basketball Drills Book 2nd Edition* and is co-editor of the following Five-Star books: *Five-Star Girls' Basketball Drill Book, My Favorite Moves: Shooting Like the Stars* and *Making the Big Plays*. Masiero has also helped compile one of Five-Star's latest books, *More Five-Star Basketball Drills* and is co-editor of this book.

Billy McNally is the head boy's varsity basketball coach and assistant director of athletics for Poly Prep School in Brooklyn, New York. McNally began his coaching career as an assistant coach for New York University. He has also been named New York City Private School Coach of the Year three times.

Grant McVay is in his fourth year as the head boy's basketball coach at Clay City High School in Clay City, Indiana. He has also worked numerous sessions for the Five-Star Basketball Camp.

Josh Merkel is currently in his third season as assistant boy's varsity at St. John's Prospect Hall in Frederick, Maryland, where has honed his coaching skills under the tutelage of Five-Star legend, Coach Bruce Kelly. Merkel has also been the head junior varsity coach for the past two seasons and spends his summers working for the Five-Star Basketball Camp.

Brad Metzger has been the Lake View Christian High School boy's varsity head coach for four years. Prior to Lake View Christian, Metzger was an assistant coach for Indiana Wesleyan University men's basketball team.

Jay Monahan is the CEO and president of the HOOPS CHAMPS, INC., and a member of the Five-Star Women's Basketball Camp staff. Monahan is a veteran high school basketball coach. His résumé includes the position of head boy's basketball coach at Blairsville High School in Pennsylvania.

Coach Biographies

Danny Nee is the head men's basketball coach at Duquesne University. He is the former head coach of the University of Nebraska and Ohio University. Nee began his coaching career as an assistant at the University of Notre Dame.

Jim O'Brien is the former men's coach at Ohio State University, where he led the Buckeyes to the 1999 NCAA Final Four. Prior to Ohio State, O'Brien had head coaching stints at Boston College and St. Bonaventure.

Dave Odom is the head coach of the University of South Carolina's men's basketball team. Odom built his legacy at Wake Forest University where he built them into one of the elite programs in the country. He is active member of the NCAA Rules Committee and the National Association of Basketball Coaches board of directors. On July 11, 2002, Coach Odom was inducted into the Five-Star Basketball Camp Hall of Fame.

Ryan Odom is the assistant men's basketball coach at Virginia Tech University. Odom's prior coaching duties include being an assistant men's basketball coach at American University in Washington, D.C., University of North Carolina at Asheville, and Furman College in Greenville, South Carolina.

Robert Pacsi is the head boys' basketball coach at Twinsburg High School in Twinsburg, Ohio. An Ohio coaching legend, Pacsi's coaching career of 33 seasons has amassed over 458 wins. A Five-Star veteran for more the 15 years, Pasci has served as resident coach, stationmaster and league commissioner.

Buzz Peterson is in his third year as head men's basketball coach at the University of Tennessee, in Knoxville, Tennessee. Peterson is the former head coach at Tulsa University, where he led the Golden Hurricanes to a NIT Championship in 2001.

Kevin Pigott is the head boy's basketball coach at the Fordham Preparatory School in the Bronx, New York. Pigott is the President of the New York City Coaches Association and a board member of the Basketball Coaches Association of New York State. Pigott has been associated with the Five-Star Basketball Camp for 15 years. He assisted in the compilation of Five-Star's most recent publication, *More Five-Star Basketball Drills* and is co-editor of this book. Coach Pigott is also a published international author.

Brandon Podgorski is a rookie Five-Star coach. Podgorski's coaching credentials include assistant boy's varsity coach of Bloomington North High School in Bloomington, Indiana, where he coached Sean May, the former Mr. Basketball Indiana and current University of North Carolina star.

Jim Psaras is the head boy's varsity basketball coach at Rogers High School in Newport, Rhode Island. Psaras led Rogers to a Rhode Island State Championship. He is a member of the National Association of Basketball Coaches and has worked at the Five-Star Basketball Camp since 1988.

Walt Ramsay is currently the assistant boy's coach at Central High School in New Jersey. Ramsay has spent the past 25 years coaching in the Shore Conference. He has also been a resident coach for the Five-Star Basketball Camp for the past seven summers.

Al Rhodes is currently the head boy's varsity coach at Logansport High School in Logansport, IN. Rhodes is also the head men's coach for the Bahamas National Team, former head boy's basketball coach at Warsaw High School and assistant men's coach at Tri-State University. A Five-Star Basketball Camp veteran, Coach Rhodes was inducted into the Five-Star Basketball Camp Hall of Fame on July 12, 2003.

Matt Ridge is the assistant boy's basketball coach at East Davidson High School in Thomasville, North Carolina. Prior to East Davidson, Ridge spent two years as an assistant coach at High Point Central High School and as a junior varsity men's basketball coach at his alma mater, the University of North Carolina. He also played two years of collegiate ball at UNC.

John Robic is entering his fifth season as head men's basketball coach at Youngstown State University in Youngstown, Ohio. Robic's coaching career began as a graduate assistant and head junior varsity coach under Coach Larry Brown at Kansas University. He was instrumental in assisting Coach John Calipari and the Minutemen of the University of Massachusetts to the 1996 NCAA Final Four.

Jim Rosborough has been the associate men's basketball coach at Arizona University for the past 15 years. Rosborough initially began his coaching career alongside Coach Lute Olson at the University of Iowa, before taking the head coaching position at Northern Illinois University. In April 2002, Rosborough was inducted into the Illinois Basketball Coaches Association Hall of Fame.

John Saintignon is the head men's basketball coach at Canyon del Oro High School in Oro Valley, Arizona. He has played professional basketball in Spain and Mexico, and had the opportunity to tryout with the NBA. Saintignon has served as a coach and director with camps such as the Five-Star Basketball Camp, Superstar Invitational, and the Michael Jordan Flight School.

Tim Saliers has 11 years of coaching experience at the collegiate level. He has led his team in Denmark to the National Championship.

Kendrick Saunders is currently the assistant men's coach at Frostburg State University in Maryland and former assistant coach at Hunter College in New York City. Sanders' hones his coaching skills during the summer by coaching at such camps as Five-Star, West Point, and Seton Hall.

David Scrivines is the varsity boy's basketball coach at Platt Tech High School in Milford, Connecticut. Scrivines is a former assistant men's coach at the University of Bridgeport and Springfield College in Springfield, Massachusetts.

Brantley Shields has served as an assistant men's basketball coach at Averett University in Danville, Virginia, for the past two seasons. He also received his bachelor's degree and is currently seeking his masters in education from Averett University. Shields is also a health and physical education instructor at Galileo Magnet High School.

Pete Smith has spent the past 20 years as a resident coach, league commissioner, and head coach at the Five-Star Basketball Camp in Pittsburgh. Smith is currently serving as assistant coach of the Bahamas National Team. In addition, Smith's head coaching experience includes stints with Manchester High School, Noblesville High School, Penn High School and Carmel High School. On three occasions, Smith has also been selected to the Indiana Basketball Coaches Association board of directors. He is presently an associate director of the Indiana Basketball Hall of Fame. He also spends time as a color basketball analyst for the HomeTown Television in Indiana and the IHSAA Radio Network

Tubby Smith is in his seventh season as head men's basketball coach at the University of Kentucky. In 1998, Smith led the Wildcats to the National Championship in just his first year at the helm. Smith's 13 years of college head coaching experience have included jobs at the University of Tulsa and the University of Georgia. He also currently serves on the National Association of Basketball Coaches Board of Directors.

Tony Staffiere is the head women's coach at Regis College in Weston, Massachusetts. Staffiere's prior duties included an assistant women's coaching position at Lemoyne College. He has also served as an assistant men's coach at Onondaga Community College, the Maine Maritime Academy and Westfield State College. Coach Staffiere has worked both the men and women's camp for Five-Star.

Bob Starkman is presently the head men's basketball coach at Broward Community College in Coconut Creek, Florida where he once coached the women's teams. Starkman has worked the Five-Star Women's Basketball Camp and has also coached the Eastern Regional Basketball AAU Club known as the Brooklyn Beasts. When Starkman is not coaching he is a U.S. customs agent and has 24 years of law enforcement experience.

Robert Strong is the head boy's basketball coach at Nature Coast Technical High School in Brooksville, Florida. His camp experience includes working at Michigan State University and Central Michigan University, as well as the Five-Star Basketball Camp.

Roberto Thompson is the head boy's basketball coach at Chinle High School, Arizona. Thompson has honed his coaching skills for the past five summers at the Five-Star Basketball Camp, serving as stationmaster and league commissioner. He is the former athletic director for the Tucson Hebrew Academy.

Sean Tyson is the assistant men's basketball coach for the Great Lakes Storm of the Continental Basketball League. He has been a consultant for two seasons with the Grand Rapids Hoops, as well as an assistant coach for the Saskatchewan Hawks of Saskatoon, Canada.

Wally Vickers is in his fourteenth year as head boy's coach at Lakota East High School and his prior head coaching duties include schools such as Indian Hill High School, Durby High School and Sycamore High School. Vickers is a former Five-Star camper and has coached at the camp for the past 12 years.

Loren Wallace has served as assistant boy's basketball coach and athletic director at Nokomis High School in Illinois, head boy's basketball coach at Lincoln High School in Illinois, Bloomington Illinois High School, and Quincy Senior High School in Quincy, Illinois. Wallace was named Who's Who of American High School Basketball Coaches in 1988-89.

Herb Welling is currently the assistant boy's varsity coach at Omaha Central High School in Omaha, Nebraska, where he has helped lead them to consecutive state tournament appearances in the past two seasons. Welling has a plethora of knowledge when it comes to basketball and has served on the Five-Star Basketball Camp summer staff since 1989, performing such duties as assistant head counselor, resident coach and director of the staff coaching clinics.

Russ Willemsen has spent the past two seasons serving as a student-assistant men's coach at Lee University in Cleveland, Tennessee.

Willis Wilson is in his twelfth season as head men's basketball coach at Rice University, where his 162 victories are the most in the history of Rice basketball. Wilson is also a former assistant coach for the Owls, where he played his collegiate ball. He has also served as an assistant coach with Coach Mike Montgomery at Stanford University.

Peter Wolf is the Santa Fe Community College assistant men's basketball coach in Santa Fe, New Mexico. In addition, Wolf has worked at numerous basketball camps around the country during the summer.

Luke Yanule is presently the head boy's sophomore basketball coach at Notre Dame High School for Boys in Niles, Illinois. Yanule has also been the assistant varsity coach for the past seven years. He has been a member of the Five-Star Basketball Camp staff for past four years.

Index

Index